YOUR HEART IN GOD'S HAND

YOUR HEART IN GOD'S HAND

Tom Montgomery

Copyright © 2021 by Tom Montgomery.

All rights reserved. No part of this book may be reproduced in any form or by any electronic or mechanical means, including information storage and retrieval systems, without permission in writing from the publisher, except by reviewers, who may quote brief passages in a review.

Editor: Kelli Levey Reynolds

ISBN: 978-1-956736-61-8 (Paperback Edition)
ISBN: 978-1-956736-62-5 (Hardcover Edition)
ISBN: 978-1-956736-60-1 (E-book Edition)

Library of Congress Control Number: 2021920457

Scripture taken from Holy Bible, New International Version®, NIV®, New Living Translation®, NLT®, Amplified Bible®, AMP® Copyright ©1973, 1978, 1984, 2011 by Biblica, Inc.® Used by permission. All rights reserved worldwide.

This is a work of creative nonfiction. The events are portrayed to the best of the author's memory. While all the stories in this book are true, some names and identifying details have been changed to protect the privacy of the people involved. Any resulting resemblance to persons living or dead is entirely coincidental and unintentional.

Book Ordering Information

Phone Number: 315 288-7939 ext. 1000 or 347-901-4920
Email: info@globalsummithouse.com
Global Summit House
www.globalsummithouse.com

Printed in the United State of America

Contents

Book Reviews
Foreword
Introduction
Synopsis
Chapter 1 15
Chapter 2 20
Chapter 3 23
Chapter 4 27
Chapter 5 33
Chapter 6 37
Chapter 7 44
Chapter 8 47
Chapter 9 50
Chapter 10 53
Chapter 11 56
Chapter 12 59
Chapter 13 63
Chapter 14 67
Chapter 15 71
Chapter 16 78
Chapter 17 83
Chapter 18 91
Chapter 19 98
Chapter 20 104

Chapter 21 109
Chapter 22 112
Chapter 23 117
Chapter 24 122
Chapter 25 128
Chapter 26 135
Summary
Biography

Book Reviews

"Tom Montgomery practices a rare form of ministry – on-the-street, immediate, and grounded in his life experiences. He connects with people in an authentic way, heart to heart, and each person he encounters is better for knowing him.

I feel certain the police officers he accompanies find peace and encouragement in his presence.

I am fortunate to have known Tom all my life – he is my uncle – but I know he has a knack for connecting instantly with everyone he meets. God created him for some special tasks here on earth."

Kelli Levey Reynolds

"I first met Tom some 30 plus years ago while I worked as a police officer. The friendship that followed twisted and turned through church, ministry, children, grandchildren and more. Perfectly? No! Tom will be the first to tell you that. What I do know is Tom is living out Philippians 3:13, 14 (ESV) "Brothers, I do not consider that I have made it on my own. But one thing I do: forgetting what lies behind and straining forward to what lies ahead, I press on toward the goal for the prize of the upward call of God in Christ Jesus".

As you read this book, watch God work. Listen as God trains Tom through life's experiences, and hear the call of Jesus as He speaks: "Come to me, all who labor and are heavy laden, and I will give you rest" (Matthew 11:28 ESV)."

Don Mansfield BCBC
Director of Chaplaincy/Senior Advocate
Family Courts

"In writing to the ancient church in Thessalonica, the apostle Paul said, "We loved you so much we were delighted not only to share with you the gospel of God, but our own lives as well" (1 Thessalonians 2:8). This is a statement Tom Montgomery could say with integrity. I've known and served alongside Tom well over a decade in an outreach to fathers. I watched him act on his intention to make the most of the last chapters of life count, and he's impacted mine and countless lives by sharing his life with others. The stories in this book are Tom's way of marveling at experiencing God's goodness in service to people."

Tommy Jordon
Executive Director
New Day Services

"Through years of making calls with police officers, Tom has seen more than his fair share of people forced to cope with some of life's hellish moments. In his new book, Tom expands the scope and shares with his readers some of the crossroad experiences of his life and of the lives of people God has brought across his path. As interesting and compelling as these stories are, they serve a greater purpose than that of a historical narrative. Tom examines them in the light of God's word to discover rich spiritual insights and directions for recovery and healing. Attentiveness to these formative events and a deep desire to hear what God is saying has given Tom a depth of wisdom that inspires and equips us as we deal with our own crises.

Your Heart in God's hand is a vivid demonstration of the words of Jesus to His disciples: "In this world you will have trouble. But take heart! I have overcome the world." (John 16:33b) NIV."

Mike Brown
Juvenile Chaplain

Foreword

"Amber, I used to love hearing your dad preach at church. He was an awesome preacher and I always loved listening to him." (from the husband of a lifelong friend).

I have watched my Dad's dedication to helping others my whole life. It might have been preaching a sermon at church or hand-delivering an insurance claim check to a family facing serious illness. I watched my parents tithe generously and give to others, even when they were not asked. Giving and helping others always has been a priority and a joy.

When dad retired, it took him a while to find a new way to help others. He eventually landed in volunteer work as a Chaplain for the Police Department. Riding out with the police during their shifts, he becomes acquainted with the officer and provides a safe place for them to share the things they experience. There also is the opportunity to comfort families when the officer is dispatched to an emergency. This helps the officer, the families and provides a place for dad to share and use his gifts of giving and caring for others.

This book is a collection of experiences recorded by someone who has spent his life devoted to using his gifts to help and bless others. In return, he will tell you he has been blessed. This is a record about how God uses us to stand in the gap for one another when we place our heart in His hand.

Amber Montgomery

Introduction

Is it possible for a well meaning person to bring comfort to someone whose world has been rocked with bad news, or is that a job for a minister or trained counselor? In 2 Corinthians 1:3, Paul referred to God as the "source of all comfort." Do we stop there or go further in order to grasp Paul's message? "He comforts us in all our troubles so that we can comfort others. When they are troubled, we will be able to give them the same comfort God has given us" (vs. 4 NLT). That sounds like an open invitation.

Hardships create challenges that can knock the props from under us. Over time, I have reached a place where I desperately want to give as effectively as I have received. Results aren't always obvious. Moses didn't live to see the result of all his work. But who is keeping score anyway? Think of the givers you know. Isn't it obvious that giving is their sweet spot?

What we are seeking is the identity God has placed in us and what He can do with us if we place our heart in His hand. Solomon wrote "The king's heart is like a stream of water directed by the Lord" (Proverbs 23:1 NLT). Satan makes every effort to divert our hearts from God's. Sadly, some go through life and miss the Lord's direction completely. Long ago I determined not to be one of them. Maybe I'm a late bloomer; but I didn't find my sweet spot at a young age. What I've learned has come the hard way, but I'm ready to go out on the move.

Gilda Radner wrote: "I wanted a perfect ending. Now I've learned the hard way that some poems don't rhyme and some stories don't have a clear beginning, middle and end. Life is about not knowing, having to change, taking the moment and making the best of it without knowing what's going to happen next: Delicious Ambiguity."

After training for the ministry and serving there for a time, I spent the next several years in insurance sales. Although my vocation was sales, one thing is clear, I never left the ministry!

Among the treasures in my library is an autographed collection of books by Og Mandino. I read every Zig Ziglar, Norman Vincent Peal, and Clement Stone book and many others. There were personal mentors who took an interest in my career transition and who taught me that motivation is essential for success. There are three principles are derived from those who have the gift of motivation. The first principle is self confidence, the second is to see value in what we do, and the third is to reject slavery to fear.

Within these pages are a collection of experiences that have shaped me over time. Although each experience recorded was real, there has been an effort to make people and places as ambiguous as possible. My own identity cannot be concealed. It really was me—walking into heart-wrenching situations behind the Heavenly Father with my heart in His hand.

The book Push the Rock by R.W. Long begins with a quote by Louis Zamperini; "Yet a part of you still believes you can fight and survive no matter what your mind knows. It's not so strange. Where there's still life, there's still hope. What happens is up to God."

You will see that I had to learn to depend on God for results. Ministering by being present is referred to in a discussion of the life of Fred Rogers. In the Bible, Job's friends sat with him for seven days without saying a word. Silent presence alone has been a frequent ally and has a way of dispelling a feeling of failure.

Proverbs 2:20 instructs us to "walk in the steps of good men." Most of us have been blessed by someone who provided inspiration and guidance. You will meet some of those God sent my way. . It's time to "pay it forward" and be that for others.

Karl Jung wrote, "Be the man through whom you wish to influence others." It is intended that these pages will reveal my passion to do so.

This effort is dedicated first to my patient and understanding wife of more than 50 years. Much time has been spent not knowing what I wanted to do "when I grow up." Brenda has supported and believed in me from the start. Dealing with uncertainties is something she does well.

Our three children (Holly Tomm, Paul Thomas, and Elizabeth Amber) have supported Dad when he was floundering, completely relying on faith and the support of their mom.

It is appropriate to mention Mother and Dad (God chose them as my parents), older sister Betty and husband Jimmie (both deceased), younger sister Judy (my struggling companion growing up) and Brother Dr. Robert Jr. and his wife Sandra (both deceased). All of these gave vital direction to a confused boy navigating his way through life.

I must acknowledge the men and women who serve as first responders everywhere. Their work is a special calling (Romans 13:1-3). I tell them they are my "post- graduate professors." Those who take me with them are younger than my children (sometimes grandchildren). At the end of the shift, gratitude is reciprocal. They are my heroes.

R.W. Long offers this: "I went forward into the darkness." This servant has grown accustomed to living that way. In every case God is found in the darkness, He turns it to light and He is good. That is my message to the hurting and those who have the heart to comfort them.

Tom Montgomery

Synopsis

Overcoming me

It probably came to a head as I watched my motorcycle loaded onto a large trailer. The man handed me a check and I stared at it for a long time. This was the culmination of many years of motorcycle riding. Of all the things I have done to gratify my cravings, motorcycle riding was at the top. This bike was a lifetime dream and I was walking away.

I've outgrown golf. A nice set of clubs sits in the garage. It is difficult to justify spending four and a half hours out of a day doing something I never did well. I gave away most of the fishing gear. There are three full cases of shotgun shells which may last until I go to heaven.

I don't feel cheated at all. There are good memories from all of these. One of my hunting friends hired a photographer and gave me a CD of a pheasant hunting trip in South Dakota. Our son went on the last trip and it was worth every penny spent.

Mark 10; 29-31 stands out in a new way. "I assure you that everyone who has given up house or brothers or sisters or mother or father or children or property for my sake and for the Good News, will receive in return a hundred times as many houses, brothers, sisters, mothers, children and property – along with persecution. And in the world to come that person will have eternal life." There is Mark 8:36: "If you try to hang on to your life, you will lose it. But if you give up your life for my sake and for the sake of the good news, you will save it.

I admit that many of the above things can qualify as self-indulgence. Often they were props I used to look like a normal guy. But I cannot make a universal case against any of them. I often played golf in fundraisers for good causes and business development. A while after retiring, I played while Brenda drove the cart. We took our grandson, Hunter, along with an extra set of clubs for him to take a few shots. He loved it and we loved being with him.

Before retiring we spent two years caring for Brenda's mother during her cancer. We would rise early on Saturday, take a ride on the motorcycle, leaving mom to sleep in. Weeks were stressful and a bike ride provided calming relief.

It's a bit of a letdown to read an obituary telling the life story of a man who was involved in everything but family. He loved hunting, fishing, motorcycles, auto racing or a certain sports team. Not much detail about family or generosity to others. Those are the things that leave a legacy. I have not done it perfectly but my children and grandchildren have memories (along with pictures) of precious moments we spent together. Children need those more than I need the other things.

Moses saw his life change when he made the decision to "refuse to be called the son of Pharaoh's daughter" (Hebrews 11:24). As the stepson of Pharaoh, Moses was a somebody. D.L. Moody wrote "Moses spent the first 40 years thinking he was a somebody. He spent the second forty hears learning he was a nobody. He spent his third 40 years discovering what God can do with a nobody."

We are not accidents. No one comes into the world merely to exist. Psalms 139:13 (NLT) makes it clear that God "made all the delicate, inner parts of my body and knit me together in my mother's womb." Finding our uniqueness honors God. Cultivating that uniqueness will enable us to touch lives in a way that will make an eternal difference. I invite you to join me in searching for our strength, honoring God and finding our part in His story.

Chapter 1

Clergy Or Layman

*"I have become all things to all people so that by
all possible means I might save some. I do all this
for the sake of the gospel, that I may share in its blessings"
– 1Cor. 9:22, 23. (NIV)*

Brenda and I made our Christian commitment a year after we were married. It was a gentleman at my work who initiated the process. He called in a report to me at the end of every shift long before we met in person. By the time we hung up, a few spiritual issues had been addressed. Months later, we were invited to his home for dinner and further discussion. Our visit a week later concluded at a church building where we committed our lives to Christ through baptism just before midnight.

Through undergraduate and graduate training, there were no classes on how to intervene at the point of tragedy in a person's life. There was no training available to equip me for this task. It is unlikely that academia ever will provide this skill. Even with the classes taken in crisis intervention since college, situations are so unpredictable, most often faith supersedes skill.

I have the privilege of working closely with the police department in a major city. The Clergy and Police Alliance is an effort to partner with the spiritual leaders in the community who assist police officers by being with them on calls to offer comfort at times of tragedy. We are called to the scene when special intervention is needed. It is humbling to experience what the officer experiences during his day. A large percentage of time is spent flowing through the city, creating a police presence. At other times we speed through neighborhoods with lights flashing and siren blaring. That can be a bit unnerving.

On most calls, details are sketchy. The dispatcher only can relate what the caller tells, and many details often are missing. What is known is there soon will be an encounter with someone experiencing trauma of some kind. On the way to the scene, divine guidance is sought for the appropriate words and heart to reach out and offer comfort.

What Are The Words?
What can be said to a grandparent who has checked on a sleeping grandchild and found the child deceased? The grandparents were rearing this child and siblings.

Where are words for a wife who has found her husband deceased on the living room floor? He was watching television when she told him "good night" just a few hours before. His son gave a hopeless look and said, "I didn't even get to tell him goodbye." The fishing boat in the driveway was a clue. "Did you fish a lot with your dad?"

"Oh yes, but now what am I doing to do?"

Where are the words for a wife who shares children with her husband? Stress of unemployment and job rejection had taken their toll. She drove home from work to see why he was not answering his phone. What she found was clear evidence of the brokenness of our world: his lifeless body in their bedroom – the result of a self-inflicted wound. The officer introduced me to the wife and I probed with questions, just to get her to talk. She was in shock and her emotions needed an outlet.

How do I approach a man sitting on the bedroom floor next to his deceased wife, crying as he holds her hand? "We cannot get him to move," the officer said. Officials were on their way and needed to have clear access to the deceased. I had my work cut out for me. I took my place on the floor next to the husband, after asking his permission. With my arm around him, I asked him to tell me what he could about what led up to this situation with his wife. I listened.

Then I asked, "Have you and your wife shared a belief in God?"
He struggled to speak the word, "Yes."
"Would it be OK with you if I say a prayer?"
He replied, "Yes."

His sobbing overpowered my words. The room was full of family and friends. They were silent.

This was not the result of training or pastoral experience. It came directly from God. The words were His as well.

How does one talk with a traumatized boy, barely a teen, who was the only eyewitness to a homicide less than an hour before? The deceased lay in a driveway across from the boy's house. The boy was peeking through the blinds when shots were fired. I received a description of what he saw. He already had given details to several police officers. Each time he recalled a little more. I encourage him to talk freely to the officers so they could help the family of his neighbor when they arrive. Now I am listening to his fears. His question was "How can I feel safe?" Together we explore ways to feel safe and handle the vision he will carry in his mind for the rest of his life. Still a youngster, he has experienced something that few people will, regardless of how long they live.

Soon after officials arrive on scene, news crews appear with their vans, antennae, and cameras. Before the investigative work is far along, networks have reported the event with as many pictures as they can gather. The report is aired and doors are checked before calling it a day. Not much thought is given to the event after that. But the youngster's mind was destined to dwell on this night for years to come.

The nightly news can be depressing. People make bad choices and those choices hurt others. It happened with the first brothers, Cain and Abel. Abel didn't deserve to be killed – especially by his own brother. But Satan asserted his presence from the very beginning. He still does.

Question

How did Adam and Eve deal with this? They didn't have access to Philippians 4:13: "I can do all things through Christ who strengthens me." Not only did they face the death of a son, their other son committed the crime – and fled.

We watch the news or read the reports, shrug and go about our lives, happy that tragedy has not hit our family. That may be a bit pharisaical, but our time will come. We will face extreme heartbreak. Personal heartache and the comfort we receive make our efforts more effective to walk through such experiences with others.

"Praise be to the God and Father of our Lord Jesus Christ, the Father of all comfort, who comforts us in all our troubles so that we can comfort those in any trouble with the comfort we ourselves receive from God." (2 Corinthians 1:3, 4 NIV).

Dallas Willard describes the "striking availability of God to meet present human needs through our actions." Brenda and I have been on the receiving end of "God's availability" through another person who was at the right place at the right time. We live with a consciousness of giving back. Life's challenges are too hard to just "suck it up and take it like an adult." The God who created us "knows how we are formed, he remembers that we are dust"(Psalms 103:14). He is the master comforter and teacher.

Our Identity Is Not Our Own

I am the sum total of pieces of a number of good people. Jesus is at the top of my list of heroes. He was (and still is) the master of loving people. He loved good people, sinful people, downright evil people, and hurting people. There is no more effective way I can model the behavior of my favorite hero than to love everyone all the time.

God graciously placed several role models in my path. None of them did it right all the time – but Jesus did. Scores of people have been thanked for their influence. Most of them are caught off guard. They never knew they were being watched being a good example until they were told. Colossians 3:15 tells us to "be thankful."(NIV) Many are thanked – including Jesus – who places me in situations where I can come one step closer to relating to others with a heart like Him.

If you can possibly identify with me through these opening remarks, you can receive a glimpse of my heart's desire to return the comfort that has been received. This is an effort to 1. Communicate (through real experiences) the need for someone to be available to a hurting person. Trauma does not arrive at a convenient time. Also, it is an encouragement to 2. Be willing to allow God to shape us into the character that brings Him glory – even if it is painful at times.

Chapter 2

Handling Trials– When They Hit Close To Home

A Vietnam veteran envisioned sitting in a circle with others. Challenges are placed in the middle with the offer to trade with someone else. No one would be willing to trade with anyone else.

Not many would want to trade their woes for those of someone else. When we gain insight into the lives of others, we are led to prefer our own. Each heartache that we have endured has contributed to the person we are today. It remains a mystery what "me "would look like after living through the trials of someone else.

The untimely death of a loved one catches us off guard.

In 1973, on his 42nd birthday, my only brother lost his life very early in the morning. It was a head-on collision that also took the life of the other driver. Brother had practiced veterinary medicine 14 years and had a wife and two young daughters. The oldest daughter was set to graduate high school in a few days. His physician friend received the call and went to the house with the news. We didn't hear until the next morning. My heart has ached all these years for my sister-in-law and two nieces. That moment of trauma changed their lives. Mine, too.

Questioning Our Effectiveness

When someone is facing a burden and we are called to intervene, it is common to question our effectiveness. A chaplain who has spent years dealing with people in trauma offers this advice:" If you ever feel confident going into a situation like that, it might be time to quit." I speak with the family of a homicide victim as they arrive on scene. My heart connects with the mother. This is the woman who carried the child until birth. She poured her life into the child as he grew. This is far from anything she wanted. The older brother arrives, remembering all the times he protected him as they grew. This time he wasn't there to help.

In another instance, family issues were impacting the children. Dad was called to the school of the youngest. The child was having an emotional reaction to an illness and needed medical attention. As they drove to the emergency room, the child passed away – in the vehicle next to dad.

A widower related a difficult memory as we talked outside an assisted living center. A phone call informed him that his son (in his 30's) had taken his own life in the back yard of their home. The death of his mother was too much for him.

A gentleman driving home from work was passing the scene of a horrible accident. His wife's car was being loaded on a wrecker, but she was nowhere around. Near a curb he recognized a shoe that belonged to her. Thoughts raced through his mind. First responders (and even onlookers) had left the scene and there was no one to ask about details. After searching he found her alive but seriously injured. Those few minutes of not knowing were the most agonizing of his life. It was a powerful time of reflection. He recalled the last unkind word he had said to her, along with other acts of impatience, judgment, and thoughtlessness. He had plenty of time to regret them all and plan a path of healing.

There are those who will get through this life without much pain. Issues that consume them will be: 1. Is the lawn mowed? 2. Are the bills paid on time? 3. Will my car start when I turn the key? There are a host of things that require little strength or endurance. My sister-in-law is no longer dealing with my brother's death. She has been gone for many years. So have our parents. My brother's death was the only time I saw my dad cry. As years passed, the family adjusted, children were born, grandchildren were added, and careers changed. That event was a catalyst that forced the family to refocus. Many new things have eclipsed and overshadowed that single event that brought so much pain at the time. It has been evidence that life goes on and survival is possible. Every life has meaning. It is when a bad choice (or no choice at all) is made that a person's destiny can be short-changed and leave their family missing out on a great deal.

Chapter 3

Where Is God?

"Consider it pure joy, my brothers and sisters, whenever you face trials of many kinds, because you know that the testing of your faith produces perseverance." (James 1:2,3) NIV.

If we are honest, trauma can shake us to the point of feeling abandoned by the God we have trusted in the past. In the midst of my own pain, I confess that sometimes worship has been difficult. With a heart crushed, other worshippers appear to be singing with far more joy.

Not all the Psalms were written by David. Psalms 78 was written by Asaph. Asaph was a Levite in the court of King David as well as a music leader and teacher. He spent 72 verses encouraging God's people by reminding them of how God protected and led His people in the past. It is striking that Asaph was detailing events for which he was not an eyewitness. These events happened hundreds of years before his generation. Yet he told about them in detail, in order to support his claim that God is reliable, aware,and works on behalf of His people. It is a constant theme throughout scripture. Asaph wanted his readers to recall the accounts of how God walked with His people. If He can do that for them, He can do it for us. Count on it.

We can look back and recall how God was in the middle of our own experiences. Brenda and I have been married a long time and have faced some very difficult experiences. Though our trust sometimes weakened, God always was there.

All our children have blessed us from the beginning. Our youngest provided an experience that demonstrated God's presence in difficulty. Four months after her birth, we were in the doctor's office for a regular visit. I pointed out something that I already had shown Brenda. Her head was not symmetrical and one eye socket was larger than the other. We were hoping it was normal and would correct itself.

The doctor told us that he would like for us to take the baby to a neurologist, but those in his referral base would put us months away from a visit. We were placed on a waiting list with no idea what we were facing. I was discussing this with one of my good friends from graduate school. He said his wife's brother was a neurologist. "Let me see what I can do." He called me back the same day with an appointment.

We did not even check our calendars. The date and time were noted along with a commitment to be there. An anticipated six-month wait turned into only a few days. Then came one of the most difficult things I ever have done. I carried our little 4-month-old daughter toward the operating room of a hospital in Saint Paul, Minnesota, handed her to the anesthesiologist and sat outside the door of that room with Brenda, while a neurosurgeon operated on her for a Coronal Craniosynostosis.

We would have preferred dealing with colic or allergies. God saw us through this with a great deal of prayer and strength that we gained from one another. After the surgery, the surgeon emerged from the operating room as our child screamed from inside. We were certain she wanted us. The surgeon anticipated our fear and said, "That's normal. She is waking up. She did fine and will be fine." Maybe she was fine-but we were not.

I was in good company. David wrote in Psalms 13 (NIV):

"O Lord, how long will you forget me? Forever?
How long will you look the other way?
How long must I struggle with anguish in my soul?
With sorrow in my heart every day?
How long will my enemy have the upper hand?"

David was confident of moving beyond his pain. "But I trust in your unfailing love. I will rejoice because you have rescued me. I will sing to the Lord because He is good to me." David had confidence: "I will rejoice, I will sing." Somehow David knew he would not feel abandoned for long. God had come through before and He will again. Been there, done that, but not so easy when the chips are down.

Listening

> *"Understand this, my dear brothers and sisters:*
> *You must all be quick to listen, slow to speak…." (James 1:19 NLT)*

Brenda shared with me a conversation she had with a lady whom she had never met. As they walked beside one another, Brenda asked her about her day. The lady shared her story. Two months earlier, she had been driving her daughter to the doctor when her daughter slumped over in the seat beside her. She called 911, an ambulance met her, and the daughter was transported to the hospital. The lady called her grandson to notify him about his mom. He got on his motorcycle and on the way had a terrible accident that took his life. If James could place an arm around this lady, what would he say? James 1:2 (NIV) is quite a challenge: "Consider it pure joy, my brothers and sisters, whenever you face trials of many kinds, because you know that the testing of your faith produces perseverance." Joy? Really? Joy and trials just don't seem to be a good match.

Brenda asked this dear lady how she found strength to face this tragedy. Experiencing the death of two loved ones two hours apart would qualify as a "trial." Her answer: "God will get me through it."

In order to find that level of confidence, an eternal perspective is essential. One of my favorite teachers compares life in this world to sailing on a battle ship as opposed to a cruise ship. Romans 8:21 promises "…Creation itself will be liberated from its bondage to decay and brought into the freedom and glory of the children of God." (NIV)

Pain, loneliness, disappointment, and even heart-wrenching pain are part of life. This mother and grandmother expressed confidence in the promise from the heavenly Father. "Your daughter and grandson are with me." That's our goal anyway – right? Paul wrote "*to be absent from the body is to be at home with the Lord* (2 Corinthians 5:8). That is the comfort Brenda and I have used for over 30 years regarding our second grandchild. Tyler did not live on this earth three months. We have the assurance that he is "at home with the lord." We have been comforted countless times by others who listened to the outpouring of our hearts over Tyler. We long to provide the same comfort for others.

It made no sense to Job that his life was disrupted the way it was. Neither he (nor his children) had done anything to deserve death. The book begins by declaring that "This man was blameless and upright; he feared God and shunned evil." (Job 1:1) When his children were taken, along with his significant possessions, his wife suggested that he "curse God and die." (Job 2:9) His immediate response was honorable: "Shall we accept good from God and not trouble" (Verse 10)?

We have been dispatched by our maker as "sheep among wolves" (Matthew 10:16). If David sometimes felt alone, then I am in good company. But David had confidence in God's deliverance. We have, too. Our Shepherd has sent us out but not without resources.

God is in the middle of our heart-wrenching pain. He feels it with us. But He never apologizes for permitting us to endure it. He didn't do it for Job and we can't expect his apology, either. Brenda and I know the value of a good listener, and we desperately want to have the heart of a listener.

Chapter 4

"This High Priest of ours understands our weaknesses, for he faced all the same testing we do, yet he did not sin."
– Hebrews 4:15 (NLT)

"Easy for YOU to say. You're not feeling what I'm feeling." Isn't that our sentiment when someone offers a trite word of comfort in the midst of our pain? There are certain things that we don't learn in a counseling course. Limited comfort will come in a counselor's office. Often, we come up short in our effort to comfort trauma unless we have endured a similar experience.

Jesus provides ultimate credibility. Hebrews 4:16 encourages us to "approach God's throne of grace with confidence, so that we may receive mercy and find grace to help us in our time of need." Still difficult? Amen to that. But Jesus is the ultimate comforter who can identify with any hurt.

A frequent one-liner in scripture is "fear not." Those are nice words, but who can say they have spent life avoiding fear. The book of Job gives a clear vision of the suffering of a good man. Job was one of those men who had everything going for him but quickly lost it all. In Job 3:25, Job declared, "What I feared has come upon me."(NIV) Here, Job admitted his fear of being separated from all the good things with which he had been blessed. They were all taken from him in a short time. No wonder it took over 40 chapters to tell his story.

I have times when I "count my blessings" and then "what if" all the scenarios. Brenda is better at this than I am. She is the one who went through a form of cancer. I am certain I fretted over the situation far more than she. Often, she reminds me that we must get the most out of each day. That is a good reminder. We know the Bible says it, but it is a different story when a person is faced with challenges with no answer of an outcome. It is far simpler to declare this from a position of comfort. We all need the confidence of David when he wrote, "The Lord will work out his plans for my life." (Psalms 138:8) (NLT)

In "The Horse and His Boy" by C.S. Lewis, the lion spared Aravis. She speaks to the Hermit: "I say! I have had luck." The Hermit replies: "Daughter, I have now lived a hundred and nine winters in this world and have never yet met any such thing as luck."

My hero doctor has a building named after him. That came at a great price, because he persisted in something he believed in, even through difficulty. What a boost to our pride and ego for a building to be named after us. It would give us some assurance that we made a recognizable contribution and added value in this world. But rather that BE him, I'm glad I KNEW him. I don't know how well I would have handled all the challenges he faced. This amazing man lived into his 90s and was so filled with humility I am certain he never (before he left) understood the full impact of his work. Future generations will receive a chance they may not have otherwise. Brenda is one of them. The building bearing his name is a medical school he began. Brenda's oncologist is a graduate.

Moses did a great deal in leading the Israelites out of Egypt, through 40 years in the desert and to the brink of the Promised Land. He did all this work, only to be told he would not experience it himself. God took him to a high place to see it from a distance. His life on earth ended at age 120 without experiencing the result of the work he was called to do. He continues to receive credit in scripture, even though he is not around to hear. I will be satisfied having my name printed on the hearts of those who loved me in this life. I cannot think of a better legacy.

Dealing With Fear

A while back, I was facing a medical procedure with my heart. I was discussing this with a doctor I met at the gym. Sharing my lack of confidence, I told him what I heard in the office of my cardiologist in their effort to calm my fears. "We do this every day." My new friend said "Yes, but it's not their heart." Wow! Did that hit home. The procedure is history and perhaps comfort and assurance can be offered to someone facing a similar procedure.

Like most, I have experienced ultimate examples of credibility. Our oldest daughter, Holly, was at our home with her children. Her 2-month-old son was sleeping in a crib that we kept. When she made a routine check on the child she found him cold, blue in color and unresponsive. She began CPR, called 911, and a transport helicopter was dispatched. The family piled into the car and raced to the children's hospital. The baby did not survive.

The funeral home was packed with friends and family offering support. Holly and I were on our knees looking at the remains of this beautiful boy, wondering what kind of man he might have been had he lived to be an adult. A lady from church walked up behind us with a photo album in her hand. She asked, "Can I share some photos of my baby who died?" The entire situation changed from that point on. No Bible quotes. No feeble attempts at encouraging words – just someone reaching out with their heart. Who could question this lady's credibility?

Brenda went through some brutal chemotherapy. I searched for some helpful reading so I could be an effective caregiver. Lessons came from others that I could never have learned on my own. There were gracious friends who had gone through similar experiences and offered comfort. We also received many hugs from medical personnel who administered her treatments. Contact continues with several of them. I listened with the intent to learn. She needed me to be fully present. I found myself resting my hand on her back during the night, following every breath for assurance of life. Those facing fear of the unknown are blessed by others who are fully present with their heart.

Listening With Compassion

Kenny was my lifelong friend and I treasure his memory. After a 20-year break from cancer, it returned. Inserting a port turned out to be a terrible experience. He was placed in Intensive Care for the night. He knew what I had gone through with Brenda. He talked and I listened.

There are times when I feel most inadequate. I bent over and put my hand on a woman's shoulder. Minutes before the police officer and I arrived, she had been told by the hospital staff that her son did not survive the gunshot. There was no assurance I could offer anything of value – but I wanted to try. I've not experienced anything similar and cannot relate first-hand. I was warned she had been disrespectful to the hospital chaplains who attempted to console her. This was one of those times I sought God's guidance to overcome the message of inadequacy being shouted by Satan. God had the experience of seeing His son's life taken unjustly. I don't recall what I said, but fear subsided when this mother reached up, gently holding my hand and saying, "Thank you. Thank you for coming." The police officers observing were a bit amazed, as well.

Our Sorrows Are Nothing New

David was described as "a man after God's heart." (1 Samuel 13:14) Yet he was just as subject to inappropriate behavior as anyone. Nathan the prophet confronted him with a four words: "You are the man." (2 Samuel 12:7). In response, David wrote one of his most moving Psalms (51). It chokes me up to read it. David had a way of returning to God when he stumbled and needed comfort. He knew it was safe there.

The account of David's son Amnon violating his half-sister Tamar is a captivating story of a parent caught in the middle. It is recorded in 2 Samuel 13. David was the father of both. This was a situation with no closure. Tamar was violated by her half-brother, changing the family dynamic forever. With good intentions, David directed Tamar to help her brother through an illness. It was a fake illness and part of Amnon's plan to violate his sister. Without knowing it, David assisted Amnon in carrying out his evil plan. "When King David heard all of this, he was furious." (Verse 21)

He had committed an indiscretion with Bathsheba, yet was unable to instill good judgment in his own son. A meaningful Psalm is 108:12,13 (NIV). David placed the victory where it belongs. It is not our ability to "suck it up" or "be strong." David asks God "Give us aid against the enemy, for human help is worthless." He then expresses confidence in God's role: "With God we will gain the victory, and He will trample down our enemies."

Absalom, David's other son, waited patiently for two years to find an opportunity to kill his half-brother Amnon for what he did. Jonadab announced to David that Amnon had been killed and, "the king's sons came in, wailing loudly. The king, too, and all his attendants wept very bitterly with them." (2 Samuel 13:36) (NLT) One might think David would rejoice over the death of Amnon for the evil he had done. Not so. He was angry over his behavior, but grieved over his death.

Have you ever wondered why God doesn't save extreme situations for those who do not walk with Him? Let the bad people suffer and leave the good folks alone. That thought crossed David's mind when he declared, "O God, if only you would destroy the wicked!" (Psalms 139:19) No wonder David questioned God's presence in Psalms 13: "O Lord, how long will you forget me? Forever?" (v.1) Most of us will feel abandoned by God sometime during our walk on earth. But David knew there is hope: "But I trust in your unfailing love." (v5)

It's easy to think we are the only ones troubled with unwelcomed events. Been there, done that. Psalms 73:7 records David's perception that everyone (even the unruly) has it made with ease and success – except him. Hebrews 4:15 offers us assurance that (through Jesus) our Heavenly Father can fully relate to the issues we face in life. God is responsible for Jesus being here. He also is responsible for those who mistreated Jesus and put Him to death. It is stunning to contemplate the heart of a Father of whom Jesus said, "My God, My God, why have you forsaken me?" Matthew 27:46 (NIV) Could God have intervened and prevented His son from suffering? Of course He could have. He witnessed persecution of the Hebrew nation by their enemies, even turning away and allowing them to suffer the consequences of their choices. The assurance we enjoy today would be entirely different had He intervened.

David was not the only one who suffered when his enemies brought him to his knees. The Father witnessed the beheading of John the Baptizer. We read the account but can hardly imagine the details. God saw every move of the ax and severing of John's head. He was present at the stoning of Stephen and in the middle of the terrible suffering by the Apostle Paul, described in 2 Corinthians 4.

God invites us to take comfort in His presence. His comfort to us is our training to offer comfort to those we encounter who are hurting. He is the master teacher. 2 Corinthians 1:4.

Chapter 5

The Risk of Relationships

"The Lord is close to the broken-hearted. He rescues those whose spirits are crushed" – Psalms 34.18 (NLT)

It is possible to avoid the risk of relational pain, but aloneness is a questionable alternative. The Apostle Paul conceded that it would be fine to be single. He discussed this in 1 Corinthians 7:7, 8. He chose the single life for himself as did Jesus. If we choose to marry, we run the risk of being separated from our spouse by death – it happens to someone every day. If we choose to have children, we take that same risk – this, too, happens every day. "No one can live forever, all will die. No one can escape the power of the grave." (Psalms 89:48, NLT) So, what are the choices?

Our grandson did not live three full months. But all the years without him have not erased our memories. He smiled at me first. He was named after his grandmother. He was the second grandchild and fostered mothering instincts in his big sister, who now is the mother of three boys-and an incredible one at that. We think of Brendan Tyler every day. Would it have been better had he not come? We don't think so.

The local news reported that a 21-year old girl had passed away unexpectedly. The girl's father said, "If God had told us, when she was born, 'You can have her, but only for 21 years,' I would have accepted." Those years brought unspeakable joy in the lives of these parents, and there was no other way to experience that joy than to accept the risk.

This issue was addressed with the mother of a 24-year-old female whose life was taken by cancer. She could not imagine life without her daughter – even for a short time. The separation brings emotional pain, but she is not willing to regret bringing this precious child into the world.

In the midst of his despair, Job cursed the day of his birth. Job's birth was God's business. Our birth also was God's business. It is our choice how we use the days we are given.

Hard Lessons
Paul's life was not a party. He suffered untold pain and persecution. Prior to his Road to Damascus experience, he lived life with the upper hand. He had status in the Jewish faith and was in the majority at the stoning of Stephen. It wasn't until he "changed sides" that he began to suffer the treatment he dealt to others in the past. Amazingly, Paul learned to live life either way (Philippians 4:12).

We miss a great deal when we go straight to verse 13. It is intriguing that Paul used the word "learned." It was not something that came naturally – even for Paul. Nor will it for us. It is learned. Paul understood that what he was seeking would not be realized in this life. It is in Philippians 3:12-14 where he describes his effort to press on toward the life that matters.

Chris Kyle was a Navy Seal sniper. He served four tours in the Iraq war and was awarded several commendations for heroism and service in combat. He and a friend were killed at a gun range in 2013. A movie "American Sniper" was made based on a book by the same name.

Taya Kyle, his widow, related how she handles her fear in a Fort Worth Star-Telegram article. She said she was scared of being left alone with two young children – "Scared that if I went to the darkest place I really felt I would not come out of it, and I had to work through that and find the courage in time, to find places in times where I could let it out or it would just live there simmering under the surface forever and have me constantly on the verge of a breakdown. And if I'm super, super honest about why I think I'm OK, it's because I believe Chris is still with me. And if I really didn't think I'd ever see him again, I wouldn't make it."

She then makes a profound admission: "I'd be a fool to not live this life and see the blessings for what they are and see the beautiful people in this world who are stronger than I am and who do more things than I do and try to give back." There are blessings around us and individuals who have placed their hearts in God's hand to be a presence for those in need of comfort. Thank God for them.

Extreme Emotional Pain

It would be rare to get through this life without it. We have no choice which events come our way. We have no choice as to how or when a loved one is taken. We might think it would be more acceptable to deal with a natural death than one that is accidental or unexpected.

A gentleman described years of being at his wife's side helping her through a terminal illness. When she passed, he dealt with necessary things, then went on an extended hunting trip. His grieving had been accomplished and his wife's death was no surprise.

Contrast that with a sudden separation –especially at one's own hand. The man, in his early 40's, became distraught over a troubled relationship. His parents were deceased and the relationship with his siblings had deteriorated long ago. Only an aunt and her daughter were close – and this was a step-aunt.

Psalms 34:18 (NLT) was a passage familiar to both: "The Lord is close to the brokenhearted; he rescues those whose spirits are crushed." As officers were with the deceased, time was spent time discussing its relevance to the situation. The family was comforted by that verse.

Gary Thomas wrote, "Read through the entire Bible, and I promise you, you won't find one reference to a 'crown in heaven' that goes to the person who had the 'happiest' life on earth. That reward just doesn't exist. Nor is there a heavenly ribbon for the Christian who felt the least amount of pain."

Kahil Gibran put it this way: "It is by the depth of our sorrows that we know our joys."

Orson Wells said, "In Italy, for 30 years under the Borgias, they had warfare, terror, murder, and bloodshed, but they produced Michelangelo, Leonardo da Vinci, and the Renaissance. In Switzerland, they had brotherly love, 500 years of democracy, and peace and what did they produce? The cuckoo clock."

Philip Yancy wrote: "God neither protects Christians with a shield of health nor provides a quick, dependable solution to all suffering. Christians populate hospital wards, asylums, and hospitals in approximate proportion to the world at large."

God certainly anticipated these off-the-chart times. The scriptures are full of His promises to be with us. What He offers must be the correct remedy. After all, He made us.

Chapter 6

Do Things Really Happen For A Reason?

"The Lord is not slow in keeping his promise, as some understand slowness. Instead, He is patient with you, not wanting anyone to perish, but everyone to come to repentance." – 2 Peter 3.9 (NIV)

A true student of the Bible is convicted that it is "inspired by God and written for our learning." (2 Timothy 3:16) It serves as an "owner's manual" from the creator to those He created. We are obligated to keep scripture in context. When Moses declared that "the Lord will protect you from all sickness, He will not let you suffer from the terrible diseases you knew in Egypt," Deuteronomy 7:15(NLT) He made this promise to the Israelites and not me.

Paul wrote to the Thessalonians: "mind your own business and work with your hands." (1 Thessalonians 4:11 NIV) This is not a condemnation of accountants, lawyers, bankers, or any profession that would utilize the mind as a primary tool.

A church spent a few weeks concentrating on passages that often are taken out of context. It is sad that time is spent applying meaning to passages that is not there. We need real hope – not false hope. My childhood mind reveled in the stories Mother read to me that ended with "and they lived happily ever after." She avoided my question each time: "what happened after that?" "Happily ever after" sounds nice, but never seemed realistic.

One study that sparked a significant amount of discussion was this: "God will not give us any more than we can handle." Often, this promise is qualified this way: "God will not give us any more than He knows we can handle." As we grow in knowledge, we adjust to the fact that one or more of our convictions has taken a beating. The passage is found in 1 Corinthians 10:13: "No temptation has overtaken you except what is common to mankind. And God is faithful: he will not let you be tempted beyond what you can bear. But when you are tempted, he will provide a way out so that you can endure it."(NIV)

This passage deals with temptation, and that is Satan's job. Joseph ran from Potiphar's wife when temptation faced him. Job refused the advice of his wife to "curse God and die." Jesus resisted Satan by making the proper application of scripture in response to the enemy's incorrect use of those passages.

When our son was very young, we often appealed to James 4:7 in our Bible study time: "Resist the devil and he will flee (this was said with force) from you. Come close to God and He will come close to you."(NLT) Even a growing boy could understand who takes the initiative in our response both to God and Satan. Jesus is our "weapon" against Satan and He "stands at the door and knocks" (Revelation 3:20). The door is opened from the inside.

There is a list of passages applied incorrectly or taken out of context, but that is a discussion for another time. Raphael McManus asks: "Are you willing to live a life that honors God and reflects His character and leaves the outcome to Him?" Either He is trustworthy or He is not. Through time He has proven to be.

Pain hurts, and that hurt often is carried through an entire lifetime. Have you ever had the news given to you that someone you love has died? I often visit with a former colleague. Both of us had one brother. Both of our brothers lost their lives suddenly in auto accidents. Each time we recall our stories together, I am struck by the detail and how much compassion surfaces in us both. We are reliving those experiences years after they happened. It doesn't consume either of us, but those experiences helped shape us into who we are today.

I recall Brenda calling and telling me I needed to come home. The memory is vivid each time. Her words and my heart floated in space as she said, "Your dad called. Bob was killed last night in a car wreck." As I struggled to get my breath, Brenda put a family friend on the phone and handed it to me. She sat silently for five or ten minutes while I cried. A few years earlier, this kind woman had found her husband deceased outside where he had been washing the car. Her credibility was well established and comfort was given.

My friend with a similar memory recalls his brother's death in detail. He describes the reaction of his mother and friends, as well as his own. I know he understands my story and I understand his.

It is amazing how it works. A memorable police call was to a home of grandparents who were raising their grandchildren. One was lying in bed unresponsive. Tension was high, but the family made it through. The grandmother recalled me telling her of the death of my own grandchild and how that brought her comfort.

Paul wrote, "Are they Hebrews? So am I. Are they Israelites? So am I. Are they Abraham's descendants? So am I." (2 Corinthians 11:22) Those things Paul had in common with his readers helped him to "become all things to all men." (1 Corinthians 9:22)

Someone said it again today: "Everything that has happened to me has happened for a reason." It sounds nice, but there seems to be no biblical evidence for it. I take full responsibility for my poor behavior and am not willing to factor it in as part of the script God has for me.

It also is a struggle to consider how much God knows about the world and wonder if He might choose to eliminate some things from His knowledge. Sometimes we are quick to assume God can do anything, but He can only do things that are consistent with His will and nature. "He cannot be tempted by evil. "(Malachi 3:6), He "cannot lie."(Titus 1:2) Can He make a square with three sides or a triangle with four? Can He make a pancake that is flat only on one side?

When Abraham drew back his sword to run it through Isaac, God stopped him and said, "Now I know that you fear God, because you have not withheld from me your son, your only son" (Genesis 22:12) (NIV). It would be interesting to know why our grandson came and left in less than three months. No one has explained why some homes are spared in a wildfire and some are not. There is no explanation why some survive mass shootings and some do not. We are faced with the task of getting through difficult and unexpected tragedies as best we can and placing them into the history of our minds. We are creatures with free will, and that was a big risk on God's part. He knew that we would need a savior and began planning from the beginning.

I Don't Know

I am willing to cave a little. Perhaps there IS a purpose for what happens to us. Perhaps God DOES NOT allow us to go through anything HE KNOWS we cannot handle. After all – He is our creator. Let's talk about that.

Certainly, God had a plan for Joseph. He came from being a red-headed stepbrother to slavery to the number two person in Egypt. Four hundred and thirty years later, we see a strong nation (under the leadership of Joshua) conquering the land God committed to His people long before.

Do we have a patient God or what? Peter thought so: "With the Lord a day is like a thousand years and a thousand years are like a day. The Lord is not slow in keeping his promises, as some understand slowness. Instead, he is patient with you, not wanting anyone to perish, but everyone to come to repentance" (2 Peter 3:9) (NIV).

Grief can hold us captive or we can move through it and become better. In the heat of grief, it is next to impossible (with our finite minds) to see any purpose at all. We may never see it during our life. History can help put the pieces together. In the midst of grief, it is difficult to say, "Everything has a purpose." A safe and logical response to the question "Why me?" is simply "I don't know."

Do we know that God can make something good come out of a tragedy? YOU BET WE DO! A couple does marriage counseling individually and together. The husband's first wife suffered through years of a horrible illness then went to heaven. He speaks her praises. The current wife then speaks up and tells how much she looks forward to meeting her predecessor. So much of what her husband is today came from her godly influence.

God put Brenda in my life. It was a match that refocused me into a man after His heart. It's been a long journey of bumps and bruises. But the outcome has humbled me. If you had known us when we met, you would have seen two opposite people. The result has been astounding. We both credit God.

Another Dilemma
I'm going to make a statement, but you have no way of knowing its validity. **"When I am with someone who has experienced tragedy, I want my compassion to be genuine."**

Most of us have been on the receiving end of compassion. We can fake many things but we cannot fake compassion. Police take me into situations where true compassion is essential. Occasionally, compassion needs to be poured out to the officer. Many of the challenges Brenda and I have endured have better prepared us for those times when we stand face to face with someone who is experiencing "off the charts" pain. It is in those times that true compassion is essential.

In the book of Job, we receive insight into the spiritual world. Job did not have this preview when his world fell apart. "One day the angels came to present themselves before the Lord and Satan also came with them. The Lord said to Satan. 'Where have you come from?'

Satan answered the Lord, From roaming throughout the earth, going back and forth on it.'

Then the Lord said to Satan, 'Have you considered my servant Job? There is no one on earth like him. He is blameless and upright, a man who fears God and shuns evil.'

'Does Job fear God for nothing?' Satan replied.

'Have you not put a hedge around him and his household and everything he has? You have blessed the work of his hands, so that his flocks and herds are spread throughout the land. But stretch out your hand and strike everything he has, and he will surely curse you to your face.'

The Lord said to Satan, 'Very well, then. Everything he has is in your power, but on the man himself do not lay a finger.'"

"Then Satan went out from the presence of the Lord."

(Job 1:6-12) (NIV).

It was at this point that the bottom dropped out of Job's life. But he had no knowledge of the meeting between God and Satan. Isn't it interesting how God spoke up for Job and Satan sought to discredit him? We enter each challenge unaware of events going on in God's spiritual world. God trusted Job's character and dared Satan to discredit him. It might have worked, but Job was grounded from the beginning: "At this, Job got up and tore his robe and shaved his head. Then he fell to the ground in worship and said: "Naked I came from my mother's womb and naked I will depart. The Lord gave, and the Lord has taken away; May the name of the Lord be praised." In all this, Job did not sin by charging God with wrongdoing" (Job 1:20,21) (NIV)

This statement demonstrates Job's character. It does not describe a man with super powers to withstand anything he would encounter. Several chapters are devoted to the feeble efforts of his friends to explain why Job was suffering. Job went off into questioning God's actions and demanding an explanation for what was happening. In the end, Job reverted to his real character and responded with the same confidence God had in him. God is able to take that kind of response from us. We can be grateful for this vision of His love and patience toward us.

Tim Madigan is a freelance writer in Fort Worth. On the day after the death of Fred Rogers (February 27, 2003), Tim wrote an article recalling important details of his friendship with this good man.

Madigan's article was reprinted in the Fort Worth Star Telegram on October 25, 2017. During their friendship, Fred walked Tim through some struggles with his demons (Fred called them Furries). In a conversation mentioning cancer being experienced by one of Fred's friends, he said, "I am angry at cancer," pounding harder on the piano keys.

Fred said, "With grief there is, inevitably some times of anger, and you know, God can take our anger." Then he paused and said, "You're ministering to me, Tim. By listening, you minister to me." Listening gives comfort in God's calling. Often it is the best option at a tragic moment.

I recall the 10 minutes of silence on the phone with our friend as I learned of my brother's death. She did not speak until I did. She need not give advice on how to accept this shocking news. Listening to my crying was enough. She cried with me. Her story was well-known and there were no doubts about her credibility. She was elevated to hero status for being there at a crucial time. That took courage. God had given her a heart of compassion as a result of her own experiences.

In 1998, Fred Rogers was featured in a cover story of *Esquire Magazine*. It was a special issue on "New American Heroes."

The author (Junod) wrote of a time Mister Rogers visited a boy with cerebral palsy who was so angry about his condition that he wanted to die. During their visit, Mister Rogers had a favor to ask. "Will you pray for me?" Fred asked. The boy was dumfounded. All his life, people had been praying for him. Why would this famous man turn the tables? Mister Rogers did. From that day forward, the boy kept Mister Rogers in his prayers and he no longer talked about wanting to die.

Junod commended Mister Rogers for his use of reverse psychology "aimed to distract the boy from his suffering." "Oh, heavens no, Tom!" Fred told Junod. "I didn't ask for his prayers for him. I asked for me. I asked because I think that anyone who has gone through challenges like that must be very close to God. I asked him because I wanted his intercession."

The suggestion has been made: "We are not people with a solution. We are the presence of God." Can we accept that assignment? In the event words are appropriate, we can appeal to my Father in every way possible to make certain the words are proper and relevant.

Chapter 7

Choices Are For Life

"The only really unethical thing for you to do is for you not to take responsibility for your decisions."
- John Paul Sarte

The choices we make each day bear consequences for life. We live in a society that looks for someone to blame. We all have said and done things that have hurt someone. That gives value to grace and forgiveness.

We have been hurt by others, as well. Much time in life can be spent apologizing, asking forgiveness, and making amends. It is up to the offended person and the offender to bury the hatchet, see how they can capitalize on the experience, and go forward in the most productive way. If a good example is not available in our home, there are others around us who can provide a pattern for our lives.

Our heroes will not know they are our heroes if we don't tell them. Others have conveyed confidence in young people who are maturing and want to offer a good example for them. It is a common experience for police officers when a prisoner is being transported to jail to hear the suspect blame everyone except themselves. Often the opportunity arises to speak confidence and hope: "You are a better person than this. I will pray that you use this experience to refocus your life in a way that will make everyone who loves you proud."

Moving On

The Prime Minister of Japan came to Pearl Harbor on an important anniversary of the attack. He had been to the Punchbowl Cemetery and paid his respects. Later in the day, he met our President at the Arizona Memorial. His government had stated that their Prime Minister had no intention of apologizing for the attack. Should that concern us? If he did apologize, what would that accomplish?

The same is true for other injustices through history. It is a burden to the heart for anyone who senses a feeling of subordination because of their ethnicity. But we never need to blame someone else for our bad choices. Thank God for His grace.

Personal Tragedy

We all have made choices that have a lasting effect. Someone told of the challenges being faced over his father's choice to end his own life years earlier. His children asked him how old his father was when he died. That was simple to answer. The question was followed by: "How did he die?" It was difficult to tell his children that his father made the choice to end his own life.

Suicide has been called "the ultimate act of selfishness" or "a permanent solution for a temporary problem." It is reported that 38,000 people in the U.S. take their own lives each year. Reports indicate that 64% of all suicides are a surprise to the family. There are many situations that drive a person to this level of despair. Many families and survivors are affected by this single act on behalf of the deceased loved one. It is one of the most difficult calls made with police.

Suicide is a choice with a generational effect. If a person takes his own life, his children are four to five times more likely to make the same choice for themselves. Recently it was noted that more lives of first responders are ended in this way each year than in the line of duty. There is preparation for the heart to bring comfort to families facing this issue.. God finds hearts that are willing to be placed in His hand for on the job training.

Anyone who has been with someone they love when they draw their last breath can detail that experience years later. Often, I am called to conduct a funeral for someone never known personally. These families may have no church connection, have been inactive for some time, or their own minister is not available. They are seeking closure on the life of someone they love. Prior to the service, there is a visit with the closest family member, asking questions that help assemble thoughts that will celebrate the life of that loved one. They are asked, "Can you describe for me your last moments with your mom?" The responses are emotional. Then, "Months and years from now, when you see a picture of your mom, what thoughts will you have?" It is another emotional moment.

The choice to make the last moments meaningful will have lasting value. A dear friend related this experience: His daughter endured a long illness that eventually took her into eternity. As she was approaching the end, she called each child in the family to her. She spoke directly to each of them words of hope and confidence. My guess is that these family members will recall that experience throughout their lives, and the daughter entered heaven with a full heart.

Chapter 8

Negative Memories

"Oh the joys of those who do not follow the advice of the wicked, or stand around with sinners or join in with mockers" (Psalms 1:1).

Dad's alcoholism accounts (in part) for the rage, irresponsibility, and lack of spirituality in the home of my youth. I bear scars and my children have picked up some of these. It is clear to them that their father doesn't live as a victim and doesn't want that for them. A lot of time has been spent apologizing. At a young age, the decision was made to NOT follow in the steps of my father. I looked to other adults who lived more responsibly. Mother provided guidance as well as my older siblings, but the absence of a father created a large void.

Jess Lair wrote: "Each of our behaviors has certain immediate and inflexible consequences. Damage is done, and we may spend the rest of our life making amends."

Dad was not all bad. I met people who worked with him and gave rave reviews of his work ethic, creativity, and heart for those in need. There were times when his heart was clearly visible, and that was a reward to witness.

I'm Not Exempt From Fault

As a young husband, there are some painful memories and regrets. Our oldest daughter came along a month after our first anniversary. We were in college, living in an apartment near campus. The apartment had a swimming pool and we spent hot summer days there. I wanted to make a swimmer out of Holly and had seen how it worked for others. Some people just put their toddlers in the water and they swam naturally. It didn't work for me. I took her under the water with me and came up laughing.

Thinking she was laughing with me, it later was learned that she was chocking and terrified. As a result, this grandmother will not put her face under water in a pool today. I regret my misguided effort.

Parking at the apartment complex was side-by-side. Next to where I usually parked, a neighbor would park her car too far to the right, so that it crowded out my space. One frustrating day, I opened my door to exit but would not open enough. Out of anger, I moved my car to another location, but not before smashing my door into the car next to me. This left a sizable scratch on the neighbors' car and even a larger mark on my heart. A short while later, we bought a mobile home and moved away. I went by the apartment several times to confess, apologize, and offer to pay for repairs. We never connected. I have carried that regret with me many years and have learned new ways to handle frustration.

I could go on and on. There are hurts delivered to those inside and outside the family. The apostle Paul had them as well but thanked God "for His unspeakable gift" (2 Corinthians 9:15).

There Is No Delete Button

It is amazing to wonder how the apostle Paul dealt with his regrets. After his conversion, others recalled his background. He was able to say, "I have fulfilled my duty to God in all good conscience to this day." (Acts 23:1) He was responsible for the death of Christians; he did it in good conscience. Often in his writing, he expressed gratitude for the grace of God and once referred to himself as "the worst of sinners" (1 Timothy 1:15).

There is a "delete" button on our computer keyboard, but none available for our heart. As our children were growing, we taught them the importance of the words we speak. Once we speak hurtful words, we can't take them back – they only go in one direction. Although forgiveness is available, damage can linger for a lifetime. A great man explained it this way: "It's like driving a large nail in a telephone pole. The nail can be removed, but the hole remains."

Working with the police can provide experiences that crush the heart. This has had a way of expanding my perspective on life. Several police officers have said that crime and misbehavior are focused on about 2 percent of the population. Ninety-eight percent are fine and upstanding citizens. Satan introduced evil into the world early in human history. Two percent of the population can keep a police department busy.

The T-shirt read "It is what it is." We spend a lot of time attempting to change "what it is." But it is a hopeless endeavor. Scripture offers some strong admonitions about the kind of people we spend our time with. "Bad company corrupts good morals" (1 Corinthians 15:33); "Stay away from fools, for you won't find knowledge on their lips, (Proverbs 14:7); "Oh, the joys of those who do not follow the advice of the wicked, or stand around with sinners, or join in with mockers" (Psalms 1:1).

Toward the end of a shift with a veteran police officer, we had time to stop and eat. He shared his story. His mother was 15 when he was born. Her parents didn't think she was equipped to raise a son, so they took that responsibility. Eventually, his father married his mother and the youngster developed a close relationship with all four adults. When mother was diagnosed with a terminal illness, dad had a conversation with him about accepting the inevitable. He said, "There is nothing I can do to change things, so I must accept it, learn from it, and move forward."

We heard a similar account from the facilitator of our Bible study group. He and his wife dealt with her illness that turned out to be terminal. She took a few days to spend Grandparents' Day with their grandchildren in another state. It was the first time they had been separated since all this began. He told us that he has come face to face with the fact that there is nothing he can do to change what is. All he can do is be grateful for the good days, learn, and move forward. The T-shirt has some merit. It really "is what it is," but these experiences provide a continual training ground for our heart that God can use at crucial times.

Chapter 9

Peripheral Damage

"For whosoever finds me finds life and receives favor from the Lord. But those who miss me injure themselves" - Proverb 8:35 (NLT)

Family tension is not a new concept. Isaac and Rebecca could not celebrate a holiday with the entire family. Jacob and Esau remained separated for many years. The pain felt by these parents must have been enormous. It was much later that we see the beautiful account of Jacob reaching out to Esau and making peace. Although the story ended in a beautiful way, there were many years in which the family missed out on unity – and who knows the pain of the parents?

Our efforts at building relationships are not always healthy. We project the future without having enough information to give our projections accuracy – a host of "what if's." We consider the possibility of our own failure in the relationship. But we can have confidence that, with assurance of God's love, relationships are worth the risk.

Who Is To Blame?

Blaming others would be doing Satan a favor. His job is to "steal, kill, and destroy" (John 10:10). We could blame God. Honestly, in desperation and deep despair, most of us have considered this. That's the way it was in the time of Job. The same idea prevailed during the ministry of Jesus. His disciples asked Him, "Rabbi, why was this man born blind? Was it because of his own sins or his parents'?" John 9:3 (NLT) is in red letters because Jesus said it himself: "It was not because of his sins or his parents' sins. This happened so the power of God could be seen in him." God can use a situation that we deem unfair to bring glory to himself.

There are a host of "good men" that we can use as role models. That is the very message of Proverbs 2:20: "Walk in the steps of good men." Paul wrote, "You should imitate me as I imitate Christ" (1 Corinthians 11:1). Let's be clear. Paul would not want us to imitate ALL that he did in his life. He admitted in Romans 7 that he struggled with doing what he knew was right. But in matters where he imitated Christ, he left a good example for us.

Isn't it a fact that we want to be identified among those who have achieved success? Most of us have the desire for success but struggle with a clear vision of the concept of success.

T.D Jakes puts it this way it: "Most people are manipulated by the approval of others, the paycheck that supports them, and the lifestyle that has handcuffed them to the brass ring of perceived success."

Becoming outstanding in sports, a cheerleader, or an honor student may be out of the question. High school reunions are interesting experiences. We are no longer separated by what separated us back then. It's what we've done with our lives since then that intrigues us and what we endured to get where we are. There is the classmate showing clear evidence of Parkinson's disease. Another discusses their recent cancer treatment. Probing questions are asked about these or recent news about issues with a child or grandchild - either negative or positive. This is not being nosey. Our values have changed over the years and we have more in common with our classmates than ever before.

T.D. Jakes wrote: "…at the end of the day, all that matters in this brief vacation we take on earth is that we didn't shrink into a corner and waste the days we're given doing what we have to do rather than rising and taking on the challenge of becoming all we were created to be."

When we step up and seek to be ourselves, there are risks. Jess Lair wrote "<u>I Ain't Much Baby, but I'm All I've Got.</u>" He compared our desire for a good family to how a fine-looking car might look in our driveway. It would be a collective pat on the back for us if people could look at our children and be amazed at how well they have done. Perhaps we would impress those we know with our success as parents. Before Brenda and I married, we had extensive discussions regarding our visions and goals for a family. It is stunning how similar her visions were to mine, and they have not changed in over 50 years.

Chapter 10

Random Kindness

Is Anyone still alive from Saul's family?
If so, I want to show God's kindness to them
2 Samuel 9:3 (NLT)

World War II brought real changes to our world. Rationing was in place from the beginning. Meat was rationed for families. Mother had metal tokens that were exchanged for a limited supply of meat at the grocery store. One butcher was very generous. He never failed to hand me a hot dog. Was it because I was such a cute and nice youngster? Perhaps. His generosity and kindness made an impact on me.

Through junior high and high school, I worked at supermarkets. On the first day of my senior year, my employer called the school and left me a message. I was to report to the butcher shop when I came to work that day. It was a promotion. No more bagging groceries and carrying them out in the hot/cold weather. During the year I worked in the butcher shop, I had several opportunities to copy the kindness that had been shown me years before.

The influence of these extraordinary men continued into my adult life. There was the dairy farmer in Wisconsin. Brenda and I were stunned by his kindness. We moved to Wisconsin to plant a church. This good man had inherited the farm from his dad who passed away prematurely. He was a young single man running the farm with the help of his mother. He met a single lady who was part of the church. She had moved there to manage a retail store. She and the farmer proved to be a good match. After a while our new friend gave his life completely to Christ.

The couple bought a home in the form of a kit. Brenda and I spent many hours helping them assemble it on the farm property.

We did not own a vacuum for our home and finances were tight. A vacuum store in town allowed us to purchase a nice machine and pay over time. About halfway through the payment plan, I went to the store to make a payment. The person at the store informed me there was no balance remaining – a kind farmer had paid what was left.

There was a blinding snowstorm one winter. While the city was good about cleaning the streets, snow was pushed in front of driveways. We were snowed in. Early that morning I heard a tractor at work in our driveway. It was our friend. He took it on himself to bring his farm machine to our house and clear the driveway.

A Heart For Kindness

It was this kind of kindness that changed Saul's heart toward David. In 1 Samuel 24, David crept into a cave where Saul was preoccupied. He certainly could have killed the king. Rather he "crept in unnoticed and cut off a corner of Saul's robe." (v.4). When Saul realized David could have killed him but didn't, he "wept aloud. You are more righteous than I…You have treated me well, but I have treated you badly." (v.17).

Two chapters later, we see the account of David taking Saul's spear and water jug from the ground next to his head as he slept. David's companions urged him to kill the king. They were convinced the Lord had delivered David's enemy into his hands. But David did not have the conscience for that. When Saul realized that David had spared him a second time, he said, "Come back home, my son, and I will no longer try to harm you, for you valued my life today. I have been a fool and very, very wrong" (vs.21). Even a king can have a change of heart.

Kindness Matters

Having been on the receiving end of this issue, most of us can testify to the truth of the above declaration. The account of David and Mephibosheth is intriguing. Mephibosheth was the son of David's friend Jonathan, who was the son of King Saul. He was five when his nurse fell while running with him in her arms and Mephibosheth became disabled (2 Samuel 4). When David became king, he asked if his deceased friend Jonathan had anyone still living from the family "to whom I can show God's kindness" (2 Samuel 9:3). When he was told about Mephibosheth (lame in both feet), David vowed to him, "Don't be afraid, for I will surely show you kindness for the sake of your father Jonathan. I will restore to you all the land that belonged to your grandfather Saul, and you will always eat at my table" (2 Samuel 9:7).

David certainly did a lot of wrong, but this account is moving. David is my example to reach out to a severely disabled veteran who is alone except for the people in the assisted living facility where he lives. Steve continually repeats the words "thank you" for the smallest kindness shown him. He walks with much effort and has a very difficult time sitting or standing. I enjoy taking him to his favorite restaurant. It's quite a chore. He is very tall and his walker is so big, it barely fits in the car. He moves slowly. Getting in and out of the car is a struggle, but I am lifted by our time together. We are given ample opportunities to identify with David's heart of kindness.

We learn how to receive and be grateful. If it is more blessed to give than receive (Acts 20:35), we can get a clear picture of that principle by being a receiver every now and again. Also we learn that kindness does not need permission. If there is a need and we have the means to provide a solution, then that is a godly response (1 John 3:17, James 2:15, Proverbs 19:17, Matthew 25:35-40).

Isn't it uplifting when kindness shows up? It is a refreshing alternative to the evil that is present in our world. Also it is a great opportunity to place our heart in God's hand.

Chapter 11

How Pain Comes

"We are not necessarily doubting that God will do the best for us; we are wondering how painful the best will turn out to be." – C.S. Lewis

Daily news media contains accounts of individuals whose behavior has seriously affected their own life and those of their victims. Their photo is displayed for all to see. It is appropriate to feel empathy for the victims. It also is appropriate to turn hearts toward the family of the offender. Admittedly, our hearts have a difficult time mustering that much empathy.

We are made aware of those who make bad, impulsive and selfish choices that hurt others. Usually the victims are those whose lives were ended or damaged leaving families with enough hurt to last a lifetime.

Encountering someone who has inflicted pain to another person can generate emotions of judgment and despair. Neglect and abandonment were familiar experiences growing up. I lost count of the number of times I visited Dad in jail. Once he was being escorted to jail (before metal detectors). He pulled his pistol and fired it in the elevator leaving a significant dent in the side of the elevator. I loved him and repeatedly told him so. Yet his agenda often was more important to him than the needs of those who depended on him. We do not choose our parents and the scriptures are clear regarding honoring father and mother (Exodus 20:5).

Many are facing family issues that are foreign to what they envisioned in the beginning. It is what it is – at least that's what they say. We may or may not be able to change it. But we certainly can grow by living through the disappointment. Be assured that we are not alone. Frequent funeral services have been added to my preaching opportunities. Each time I am reminded how much life changes when death separates us from someone who has been part of our world. In fact, the entire world changes as each person leaves the world and others enter.

Biblical Fathers And Sons

We find an emotional scene in 2 Samuel 18. David has escaped harm from the rebellion of his own son. He receives what most people would consider "good news," Absalom is no longer a threat-he is dead. Yet David burst into tears. As he went, he cried, "O my son Absalom! My son, my son Absalom! If only I had died instead of you! O Absalom, my son, my son."(verse 33).

David envisioned a different direction for Absolom. Assembling a following of rebels and seeking to overthrow his father could not have been part of David's dream for his son.

Eli's sons served as priests of God. 1 Samuel 3:13 declares that "his sons are blaspheming God and he hasn't disciplined them." Hophni and Phinehas, the two sons of Eli, were killed in a battle with the Philistines (1 Samuel 4:11). When he received news that the Ark of God had been captured and his sons were dead, Eli "fell backward from his seat, broke his neck and died" (Verse 18). The passage goes on to mention the wife of Phinehas going into labor and dying during childbirth. It is stunning to witness such a reaction to bad news regarding a loved one. It happens somewhere every day.

Extended Family

Two longtime friends called days apart. Both had a reoccurrence of cancer and it was terminal. They also requested me to conduct their memorial service when the time came. That was a first. Typically, contact is made by the family after the person passes. In over forty years of ministry, this is the first time I have been asked directly by the person himself. It was difficult and an honor at the same time. Our final visits and the memorial carry emotional memories that will last a lifetime. There is an empty spot in this heart with them gone, yet a heavenly reunion is anticipated.

Jake was first to pass. He reminded me of the time that his brother was murdered in an apartment parking lot. I lived through that experience with Jake simply by listening. He followed the investigation and trial, admitting he didn't handle it well. That is a fact. There were many visits during the experience. He either would call to diffuse or I would call him seeking a progress report on his emotions. It was the same Jake all along, only with a very heavy heart. He knew the scriptures. Why can't we just assure ourselves of God's promises and brush off the effects of such events? Is it a lack of faith on our part?

Kenny already had requested that I conduct his service when the time came. I was not looking forward to that.

I learned of a young friend being treated for cancer in another city. I had made a trip to that city to work and was determined to visit my friend in the hospital. A longtime friend joined me at the hospital to visit and encourage the younger man. After our visit my fellow comforter invited me to his home for a family dinner. We were discussing the occurrence of "off the charts" challenges in life. He told of a gentleman at church who had moved to a nursing home, long before he should have. Cancer had taken the lives of his two daughters and wife. He was not prepared to be alone. Long ago my dinner host related the account of his brother being randomly shot and killed. It is difficult to fathom this same experience with two people I knew well.

Often listening is all we can offer. It is not a grand gesture, but often it is all we have. I refuse to question the effectiveness of my heart in the hand of God. We need that kind of safe place as well. It is a blessing to be a safe place for others.

Chapter 12

Amazing Pain

"For I am convinced that neither death nor life, neither angels nor demons, neither the present Nor the future, nor any powers, neither height nor depth, nor anything else in all creation, will be able to separate us from the love of God that is in Christ Jesus our Lord" –Romans 8:38,39 (NIV)

The police call it a "disturbance" and sometimes "domestic." If it involves family, it is termed "domestic disturbance". An elderly gentleman called 911. He had been robbed and roughed up-by his grandson. Officers were talking with the family and gathering information. The sergeant radioed that he had detained the suspect one street away and the rest of us hurried there. The young man was handcuffed, placed in a police car and transported to jail.

While at the residence, the grandfather was receiving attention from first responders. My heart led me to this elderly gentleman but he was surrounded by caretakers. A daughter was assured of prayer being offered on behalf of the family. This is not the behavior that a grandfather anticipates from a grandchild. We don't need to search for evidence that the world in which we live is broken.

One evening, a man approached the officer and me and requested that we take him to jail. His record revealed ample evidence to do so. He was handcuffed and placed in the back of the police car for the ride downtown. The officer slid the window open and we talked with the man the entire way. He admitted a serious drug addiction and wanted help. He had an altercation with a friend over something foolish. An effort was made to discuss something meaningful with the troubled man.

It is a great opportunity to discuss the opportunity they have to change their actions and go a different direction in life. Loving themselves as much as family (and God) loves them often gives them the motivation needed to rewrite the script of their lives. Consideration must be given to the loved ones of the person who caused damage. Someone loves that person even though they make choices that hurt others.

Behind the Badge
There are no bigger hearts anywhere than those of police officers. They spend time dealing with those who are classified as offenders in some way and see the worse of the worse. But humility prevails during their workday.

A young mother was being transported from a retail store where she was detained for shoplifting. She was caught by store security after putting up a fight. The officer talked with her about her children and learned they were staying with an older couple in her neighborhood. As the officer pulled up to the sally port of the jail, he called the coupled to explain the situation. They were not surprised. The officer asked for them to put the children on the phone. First, he spoke with them and explained that their mom had made some mistakes. He told them that she would be dealing with results of those mistakes for a while. He handed the phone to the mother. The speaker phone was enabled as she talked with her children. After she was booked, the officer and I drove to where the children were and talked with them. There was not a single despairing word regarding their mother. He assured them that she loved them and wanted to protect and provide for them. He encouraged them to be patient and love their mom. It is one of many experiences with which police spend their time.

Read the interviews with the parents of some of the worst offenders. No one discounted their love for their child. It is in that context that we begin to understand the love God has for us. We cannot misbehave enough to turn God against us. That is Paul's message in Romans 8:37-39) "nothing can ever separate us from

God's love". It is a recurring theme in exploring changes in the life of a person who thinks "I've been so bad God couldn't possibly forgive me." It is comforting to know that God's thoughts are not our thoughts (Isaiah 55:8).

It is stunning to read a victim's impact statement after a court conviction. What is anticipated is a statement of extreme pain at the hurt or loss of a loved one at the hands of the convicted. It is not uncommon to hear these individuals express bitterness toward the offender – wishing them a miserable future. That is difficult enough to take in. We cannot even begin to feel the hurt that person is feeling. But there is another victim that deserves consideration. It is the loved ones of the one convicted – the parents, grandparents, siblings, spouse and children. These people invested significant effort into the life of this individual, envisioning a better outcome. They are feeling that their efforts have been rejected and useless. Self-blame is both common and inappropriate. This person chose a different path for themselves. At this point it is irreversible.

A man in his twenties did significant damage. His parents are in a position of leadership. The comments on social media suggested that the parents should leave their positions. What would that accomplish but give Satan total victory. What is it about his failures that can be blamed on a set of good parents? It is not uncommon for parents to blame themselves for the failure of a child. It makes no sense to impose additional loss. That is exactly what Satan wants (John 20:20). Let's put things in perspective this way: "God is the father of all mankind. Do bad choices by God's children make Him a failure?"

A young man in a responsible and honored profession did some horrible things. For his crimes, he received a prison sentence in excess of 200 years. The newspaper pictured his father in the courtroom waiting for the judge to pronounce sentence. It is impossible to comprehend what is going through the father's mind in that photo. It is something the man will carry with him until he takes his final breath.

We are shocked when someone well-known and loved surfaces with a different image. Consider the accounts of famous politicians, ministers, business leaders, sports figures, educators or celebrities who have chosen an adverse path. Do we need to recall the news coverage? We hear comments from the public that this individual has violated the admiration we had for who we thought they were. Part of our own life is wiped out. What about those closest to them?

The news released video of several teen boys behaving terribly- destroying property and hurting people. Their parents reported them to the authorities. That took courage.

Another twist is the mental and emotional challenges to children of these offenders. One young mother reaches out to females caught up in sexual abuse and explained that her own father is spending the rest of his life in prison for making children his victims.

An article described the suicide of a sixteen-year-old girl. The father made suggestions to parents about being observant of a child's changes in behavior. He warned parents against pressuring a child into superior performance. It is baffling that a person can behave in such a life- changing way. It is overwhelming to the emotions to consider the pain endured by those who loved that person

Holding on to Hope

The apostle Paul spoke with hope in the verse mentioned at the beginning of this chapter. Many years of marriage have helped keep Brenda and me on the same page. We both have experienced the death of parents, a sibling and a grandchild. We have experienced job loss, disappointing choices by children and grandchildren and we share consequences from our own mistakes. Our faith has been shaken- but not lost. Together and separately, we seek to impart the message of Paul to those we touch: "Nothing can separate us from the love of God which is in Christ Jesus." Our hearts are safe in God's hand.

Chapter 13

Less than Desired

"The child will not be punished for the parents sins and the parent will not be punished for the child's sins."
(Ezekiel 18:20) (NLT)
"And he (Jacob was limping because of the injury to his hip."
(Genesis 32:30) (NLT)

It is not our thinking that is flawed. It is the response of our heart and Satan knows it. John Eldridge wrote, "Did it ever cross your mind that every thought that crosses your mind is not your own?" More than one voice speaks to us. People in our lives are not to blame for our choices. We must claim full responsibility.

Job must have been a bit of a worrier. In the midst of his suffering, he declared "What I feared has come upon me) (Job 3:25,26). We are good at worry. An abundance of Bible passages warn us that worry is not healthy and it diminishes faith. By the time a worrier projects possible outcomes, all of the possibilities have been heard and none of them were good. Some hardships we endure may be the product of misdirection and failure. We are products of imperfect humanity and we make mistakes.

Ezekiel 18:20 is a stunning statement of accountability. We have free will and can commit to live opposite from our upbringing. Even if we make a better choice, we might walk with a limp.

The account of Jacob wrestling with an angel is a great bedtime devotional for growing children. It is found in Genesis 32:22-32 and Hosea 12:4. In this account, Jacob's name was changed to "Israel," he received a blessing and is left with a hip out of joint causing him to limp for the rest of his life. We can reject a repeat of the environment in which we were raised. If we have a negative history we can make the commitment to reject our history.

The idea of walking with a limp is intriguing. Paul endured a physical issue that God refused to remove. God said, "My power is made perfect in weakness."(2 Corinthians 12:9) (NLT). If you ever have attended AA meetings with a friend, you will hear their members take full responsibility for their addictions. Strength and support get them through one day at a time, but the propensity remains. They walk with a limp. Taking up our cross is a daily effort (Luke 9:23). God never leaves us to walk alone but clearly demonstrates His power in weakness (2 Corinthians 12:9).

Overcoming the Past
We have mentioned the young mother who works with victims of sexual abuse. Her father is in prison for that crime. She has rewritten her story. A Christian teacher was raised by atheistic parents who taught him to be an atheist. He married a Christian who inspired him to study on his own and redirect his life. There are plenty of characters mentioned in scripture with messy backgrounds (Rahab for one) but changed direction to a new life of honoring God.

I served on the board of a nonprofit ministry for several years. We worked with fathers who had abandoned their children in many ways, including their refusal to pay child support which has been court mandated. Since my term expired, this organization has expanded their efforts to mothers who have distanced themselves from their children. Often these children have witnessed a life of domestic abuse in the home. This pattern can be changed and the children set on a different path.

Boys who witness domestic abuse are 2 times more likely to develop the same behavior when they have a family. One half of girls are more likely to become victims in their adult years. This is one of the most difficult police calls. We see violence: injuries on one or the other parent, broken doors, holes in walls and broken glass. This behavior is witnessed by the children yet they are relatively calm. It is normal home life. Officers and I attempt to divert their attention in some way while another officer talks with the parent who is the victim.

Making a plan and committing to it has given Brenda and me direction. We read books and attended numerous workshops on parenting. We would never claim perfection but we had more tools to work with than we would have had by just playing it by ear.

Our granddaughter reminds us of approaching birthdays for her three boys and she never is ready. As with most committed parents, memories of the children developing are precious.

"Memories in the Walls:"
When this house shall become silent
And independence calls
Precious treasures will sustain us
With memories in the walls

When we search the place for loved ones
And discover silent halls
We'll hear all the sounds of growing
From the memories in the walls.

Though the echoes will sound lonely
When the dusk of our life calls.
We'll find strength to journey forward
From the memories in the walls

We've toiled to urge them onward
Picked them up from all their falls
Kissed their hurts and made them better
Now it's memories in the walls
When thoughts are brought to visit
By the tractors and the dolls.
We spend a few quiet moments
With the memories in the walls.

Tom Montgomery

When it's time to sing our anthem
And our greatness none recalls.
We'll know our greatest purpose
From the memories in the walls.

This mother was four when her brother was found unresponsive in his crib. She attended group counseling with other children who had experienced something similar. Being a wife and mother is ingrained in her soul. The price for that training was high. Tyler is at the feet of Jesus and his nephews are headed there. It is amazing how God can develop our hearts and use them when we place them in his hand.

Chapter 14

The Tie That Binds

"I have learned how to be content with whatever I have. I know how to live with almost nothing or with everything. I have learned the secret of living in every situation, whether it is with a full stomach or empty, with plenty or little. For I can do everything through Christ, who gives me strength" Philippians 4:12,13 (NLT)

We set ourselves up for disappointment by creating expectations that we have no right to create. Many professionals have shared that "unmet expectations" is a significant cause for failure in relationships. A college professor once related a significant discovery from years of teaching and counseling. He contended that "marriages don't fail – people fail." That is true in about every kind of relationship involving two or more people.

My favorite pre-marital counseling question is "why do you want to get married"? The most common response is "because we love one another". Another answer is "we have a lot in common". Then they are encouraged to recall their answers a few years later. Will that love hold firm after the first child is born, hormonal changes occur, a child makes a bad choice or attention is focused on an ill or dying parent, grandparent or sibling? These are situations that have the potential to upstage or strengthen a relationship.

Real Life Testing

As I write this, Brenda, our daughter Amber and I are at the cancer center. We come at least once a week-sometimes more. Every third visit consists of Brenda receiving chemotherapy. The room contains over 20 lounge chairs usually filled with cancer patients sharing the same experience. We spend a large amount of time talking with other patients and their families who have endured this much longer. So far, we have not met a single person who has chosen to give up.

Any long-term marriage will produce joy as well as challenges. Living in a broken world will give us opportunity to experience both.

Following surgery on her eyes, Brenda noticed other symptoms. Thinking it might be a reaction to the recent surgery, we made a late-night visit to the emergency room. The doctor ordered x-rays and found nothing. A sonogram revealed large stones in her gallbladder. The ER doctor stressed the importance of attending to this soon.

I had visited a surgeon regarding a hernia and planned a repair. The next morning after Brenda's ER visit, I called the office of my surgeon to ask if he did surgery on gallbladders. They saw her within two days. We were sent for an immediate scan which revealed enlarged lymph nodes in the abdomen.

Brenda was very ill and admitted into the hospital through the ER. A needle biopsy revealed lymphoma. The surgeon removed her gallbladder, did a bone marrow biopsy and installed a port through the chest wall.

She was given her first round of chemotherapy while in the hospital. Then we took her home. The next day we made a follow-up visit to the office of the oncologist. The chemotherapy had totally depleted her white blood cells. That evening, her temperature rose considerably. I called the oncologist. He instructed us to take her to the ER and that likely she would be admitted.

Brenda claims Philippians 4:13 as her favorite scripture. Often it is used in times of distress. That's exactly how Paul used it. His life had been affected by his ministry and brought new challenges. The strength of Christ is not what empowers one to climb Mount Everest, or win a NASCAR championship or PGA tournament. The context here is living with what life deals us.

It is stunning to talk with a person who is receiving chemo and says, "I'm terminal." These people know the outcome of the disease that is ravaging their body but are doing what they can to get the most out of what life has left for them.

It Never Quits

A fellow patient was receiving chemo in a recliner at the cancer center. He appeared to be in his fifties he explained that his illness was terminal. His attitude was not. He was talking, laughing, and looking up things on his iPad. He explained that he had been talking with others and asking this question: "If you could write a book about your life, what would be the title"? He explained that he listened continually for what God wants him to learn from his experience. It would be difficult to take exception to this analysis. More than one voice speaks. Most everyone spends time attempting to discern which voice to tune in and which to reject.

Often these patients are very young. Their stories are intriguing but no one has given up. Everyone expresses hope. Most are surrounded by family, either by their chair on in the waiting area nearby. They have learned to deal with the situation at hand and not be jerked around by an unwelcomed experience. Challenges in life give us the opportunity to learn a new meaning to the above passage. Most of us have held the hands of family members and close friends as they endured the same thing. Whatever we may face someone nearby has faced the same and has the heart (from God) to comfort others. That is a great use of a heart in the hand of God.

Romans 8 (also written by Paul) speaks of our groaning. Certain experiences make us groan. David had every reason to groan. He was confronted by Nathan the prophet and heard the ugly truth about himself (2 Samuel 12). He had committed adultery, Bathsheba was pregnant, David arranged for the death of her husband. Uriah was a loyal soldier in David's army-how did he deserve to die? The baby born to Bathsheba died. David was the one who deserved to die. But he played a crucial role in maintaining the throne that Christ would occupy.

Where was the fairness? A married woman who was misused by a lustful king, her husband killed and her baby died. There were plenty of reasons to groan. It was strength from Christ that provided Paul with the ability to be encouraged, whether things were going well or not.

In 2 Corinthians 6 Paul discusses some of his experiences: "We have been beaten, put in prison, faced angry mobs, worked to exhaustion, endured sleepless nights and gone without food." Where did strength come through these experiences? Philippians 4:13.

In 1 Corinthians 16:9 (NLT), this same Paul described his work in Ephesus: "There is a wide-open door for a great work here, although many oppose me." Opposition is something Paul expected. He considered it an opportunity to accomplish more. It is likely that smooth sailing would not. Where did he find his courage to continue even with opposition? Philippians 4:13.

Chapter 15

How Are You?

*"Don't tell your friends about your indigestion.
How are you? is a greeting, not a question."*
Arthur Guiterman

"How are you"? That is a Southern greeting. Most of the time the response is "Fine," even if things are not fine. Who wants to be less than fine? Someone in AA might answer, "it's a good day to be sober." There is more to that question than most realize. The person who asks is not fishing for a list of everything that is troubling. Most of the time they turn and give their attention to something (or someone) else and don't even listen long enough to hear a reply.

I have some interesting ways to respond to that question:
1. Often, I don't respond at all to see how quickly they become occupied with something (or someone) else.
2. "I don't know yet."
3. "Compared to what?"
4. "I woke up this morning."
5. "I'm getting better."

The police car pulled up to the home of a family who had been caring for the man of the house. He had liver failure and had quit breathing. All efforts of first responders failed. He was in his mid-40s. This was a premature death, but there had been enough time for the family to learn to love him. We walked away listening to the wife and daughters crying loudly. They admitted that his death was partially due to his own life choices and they were facing a future with the total absence of a father and husband. The remains were next to his bed. There was his wife, daughters, and grandchildren enduring a vision that would last them for the rest of their lives. The choices he made for himself had been sealed and affected people who loved him.

Another gentleman had been married twenty years when his wife was diagnosed with cancer. In the midst of that illness, she informed him that their marriage had reached the end. He said he had learned that, in such cases, the divorce rate skyrockets. Those who have longevity are at far less risk. He was at a loss to identify a cause of the breakdown. He cared for his wife during her illness and years later, he still is puzzled.

Another dear couple had two children. They were awakened by a fire in their house. They escaped to safety outside. Watching their burning house with their children inside, instinct led the father in that direction. The area was engulfed in flames and bystanders restrained him. The children did not survive.

The father was a bitter man for a while and wanted no more children. His wife felt differently. She intentionally allowed herself to conceive and a child was born. He learned to love that new child with a special love. This was a stretch from the life of pain and bitterness he had felt. The couple became Christians, entered the ministry and did great things with their redirected family life. We became dear friends and learned a great deal from them about the value of our children. Their hearts had been placed in the hand of God.

A good Christian man and church leader impacted those around him in a good way. His job was to maintain the roads around the county with a large tractor. He did this for years without incident. But once, when he was backing his tractor, a child on a bicycle ventured behind the machine and it took the child's life. This man's gentle spirit was unmistakable. He spent his days looking for opportunities to help others rather than waiting to be asked. A tragic situation turned into a blessing for people who crossed his path. My family carries the blessing of this man's kindness. Clearly, he had placed his heart in the hand of God.

One memorable police call involved a military man in his early twenties. His carelessly driven car struck another car and took the life of an older man. Talking with the mother of this driver certainly revealed the heart of a mom in unfamiliar territory. She related how her son had excelled in the military. He was sitting near the wreckage and the deceased victim. She asked if we could pray for her son. This was done in the midst of a crowd of onlookers and family of the deceased. A field sobriety test indicated the young man needed to be transported. My heart still aches for this young mother. It is far from what she hoped and planned for her son.

I was dispatched to the scene where a female driver had stuck a pedestrian crossing a busy and dark roadway. The officers on scene gave a detailed description then directed me to the driver. She had two family members with her and was shaking very badly. The officers commended her to me for stopping and calling for help. The commendation and compliments were conveyed to her and thanks to her family members for being with her. Few will feel qualified to address an individual in such instances. But we know with certainty that painful experiences can train our hearts and God always is there to provide the words and actions.

Real Life Application is Not without Challenge
Read the parable of the Pharisee and Publican. How many of us can identify with this character? Have you looked at the church bulletin, news story or obituary column with a heart similar to the Pharisee? It is appropriate to utter a prayer for those mentioned as ill or separated by death from a loved one. But caution must be given that gratitude is the only emotion expressed for blessings health and life in our family. Satan can be deceitful in presenting a "right to life and health" attitude and tempting us to feel superior to the people who are suffering similar to the Pharisee.

Brenda and I spent several days in the hospital room with our infant daughter following surgery. The roommate was a young girl who was there when we came and remained when we left. She was being tested for a disease that recently had been discovered.

Brenda and the girl's mother talked endlessly. Brenda and the other mom corresponded by mail for a long time until we were assured the young girl had recovered. The effort to keep in touch brought closure to an experience that was stressful for both families.

The lady I met on a visit to another state told me she was a book editor. When I mentioned to her that I was working on writing a book, she asked me what it was about. I explained that it dealt with "off the charts experiences and how we may or may not deal with them and learn." She replied, "Let me tell you our story." I braced for this.

She and her husband have a daughter who developed a very large tumor. The daughter barely was in her teens. Because hospitals were crowded, they were sent to children's hospital miles away from home. There they encountered other children being treated for cancer. When they were informed that their daughter had a benign and removable tumor, she was grateful, knowing full well that other parents were not experiencing the same outcome. She had formed a relationship with the mother of her daughter's roommate. They were dismissed and went home while the other mother waited for the diagnoses of her child. Not following up with the mother has given her something to regret since then.

The Reaper Speaks
The reaper makes his daily round
To this good earth below.
And frequently with those he's found
I see someone I know

He speaks to me when he comes near
I often hear him say.
"I'm not the one whom you should fear
It's not your turn today."

"Treasure life" his voice is felt,
"And let this be a clue.

Today I'm here for someone else,
Someday I'll come for you."

The reaper makes his daily rounds
And makes sure that I know
That where he leads me time abounds
But now's the time to grow.

The couple has faced extreme illness with their oldest son. He was diagnosed with cancer as an infant. How do we wrap our hearts around such a situation? Is it possible to become pharisaical? God is the master of comfort and opens doors for us to join Him in delivering it to those in need (2 Corinthians 1:3). It is an honor to partner with the God of heaven and experience comfort whether we are the one needing comfort or the one offering it?

Where is God?
God is sovereign and has power to bring an end to human suffering. But He watched His son suffer unjustly. When the Father speaks we can rest assured that He speaks from experience. We are not enduring anything He has not.

Brenda went through cancer treatment. Often, we were asked how things were going. The most comforting thing anyone could do was to listen to every word that we spoke. There were a few gracious folks who would ask for a report, focus on us and ask questions for clarity. There were times when we needed to talk to diffuse our feelings. At the beginning of Brenda's ordeal, she was not aware of some of her visitors. Neither did she know that some of them paused in the hall or in the room and prayed for her and for the family. She knows now.

Often it is unclear what a person means when they say, "I'll be praying for you." It would be more comforting to hear them say "My wife and I were praying this morning and specifically asked God to take charge of this situation and bring comfort and healing. We also asked God to give you hope, comfort and strength."

It is a puzzle to explain different outcomes to our requests. Even Jesus said to the Father "If it be possible, let this cup pass from me." But it was part of God's plan from the beginning and Jesus knew that history had pointed to what He was about to face. His request for another way demonstrated His humanity.

The most difficult issue for the defense of God's existence is the presence of suffering. If God exists and He is all powerful, why does He not eliminate the inequity of these issues among humans? Sickness and hardship can be brutal. Jesus suffered terribly but remained obedient and on mission for a larger purpose. The apostles were not deterred by the hardships they faced. Paul, for example, saw beyond it. He wrote "I press on to reach the end of the race and receive the heavenly prize for which God, through Christ Jesus, is calling us" (Philippians 3:14). That same promise is there for us. In the meantime, He can do remarkable things with our hearts if we place them in His hand.

Mother's Relief

The plane landed at Edwards Air Force Base in California. It was a 36-hour trip from Japan. Time was extended due to engine failure between Honolulu and the mainland. We returned to Honolulu, changed planes and left again.

It was cold in Northern California, even in August, but no one cared. We were on U.S. soil. After two years in Japan, home dominated our thoughts. One fellow passenger dropped to his knees and kissed the ground. I walked around him and headed for the nearest pay phone. After placing the collect call to Mother, she began to sob loudly. Braced for bad news, she stopped and said, "I've had two sons go overseas, and both came home safely." Other parents prayed for the same thing but to no avail.

At the end of the first year in a two-year intense ministerial training program, the teacher walked into the room. He was the one to walk us through the book of Job next school year. He gave us our summer assignment. We were to read the book 10 times during the summer. By the end of summer, Job took on new meaning.

Brenda and I have refocused on how to respond to someone who is going through a difficult time. One friend asks specific questions, then grabs a hand and prays aloud right where he is. Now we lift a troubled person in prayer immediately and avoid making a promise that might not be kept. It is appropriate to ask, "How did you feel when you first learned of this?" or "How did your spouse take the news?" or "How did the talk with the kids go?" Eye contact is made and their words capture our attention until they finish talking. We thank God for that lesson.

We love others. That is why we hurt when they hurt. Brenda and I have prayed separately and together until it seems we run out of words. Romans 8:26 (NIV) assures us that "the spirit itself intercedes for us through wordless groans." The original language of Scripture assures us that when we pray, we are not alone. We have the Holy Spirit interceding alongside us.

The vision is that we grab one end of the table, the Holy Spirit grabs the other end and we lift together. When we bring our sincere requests before God on behalf of someone we love, we are comforted knowing we had help, even though we might feel that our words are inadequate. When we cannot produce words that seem appropriate it is okay. God can hear our hearts, even without words. Jesus is our ally. "Since he himself has gone through suffering and testing, he is able to help us when we are being tested" (Hebrews 2:18) (NLT). He is amazing.

I am okay if you don't ask me "how are you"? Just say "nice to see you, Tom."

Chapter 16

Motivation to Continue

"Direct your children onto the right path, and when they are older, they will not leave it." Proverbs 22:6 (NLT)

Expectations test relationships even when it comes to rearing children. A school resource officer revealed the discovery of illegal drugs confiscated from middle school students with whom he spends his days. He went on to explain that illegal drugs had been discovered among second graders given to them by their fathers.

Early in ministry we were in a discussion at church regarding scriptural principals regarding child rearing. Proverbs 22:6 sounds like some kind of guarantee. God had Ezekiel record a significant principle in 18:20 (NLT). "The child will not be punished for the parent's sins and the parent will not be punished for the child's sins." There was a divine warning that a parent's efforts might fail since children are given free will.

During our discussion, a well-meaning church lady spoke up and declared "raising children is like buttoning a shirt. If you start out with the right button, the task will conclude the way it should." The older my children became, the more humble I became as a parent. If the right effort produced the right results then God's qualification as a father would be questionable. Consider the bad choices of humans through the ages with the ultimate parent.

What Is Our Part?

Jess Lair stated "we cannot raise a child. We only can sponsor them." Proverbs 22:6 has been translated this way: "…train up a child in the way he should go (and in keeping with his individual gift or bent"(Amplified Bible) That takes some insight by a parent. The apostle Paul put the blame where it belongs. "All have sinned and fall sort of the glory of God" (Romans 3:23) (NIV). A parent only can do what God instructs. The rest is up to the offspring. Many good parents are crushed by choices made by one or more of their children. We live in God's grace and are born with free will. There are no guarantees. That is the risk a parent takes.

As this is written, suicide has risen locally among children – some as young as 6. We are experiencing challenges to our understanding of normal. Kids are out of their comfort zone. According to the National Fatherhood Initiative, more than 1 in 4 "live without a father in the home." The report shows that such homes are 4 times greater to experience poverty, behavioral problems, and twice the risk of infant mortality, end up in prison, commit crime, become pregnant as a teen, face abuse and neglect, abuse drugs and alcohol, twice as likely to face obesity and drop out of high school. It is not a favorable picture when families deviate from God's pattern.

Most of us have made a few choices in life that we regret. These were contrary to what parents had taught. There is no way parents can be blamed for those choices or the consequences. I was careful that mother never learned of some. Thankfully many of the growing years were spent making it up to her with choices and behavior that made her proud. Her vision for her children was clear. It involved a spiritual perspective from the God to whom she introduced us and placed our hearts in His hand.

Which Way?

The master story teller Paul Harvey told of two brothers. One became a physician and the other served most of his life in prison. Interviewed individually, the question was asked was "To what in your life would you attribute your motivation to turn out the way you have?" The physician answered, "How could I have turned out any different with the parents I had?" The other brother gave the same answer.

Someone might conclude that the parents favored one child over the other. In the biblical account of Jacob and Esau the father and mother were not on the same page. In the long run we learn more about forgiveness and peacemaking from this story. Some children become stellar adults, even though their parents kept their own agenda with little attention to nurturing their offspring. Also, there are parents with broken hearts who have poured themselves into their children, only to see them go in directions that were never envisioned.

A nurse related an account that had a happy ending. Throughout her education, her father thought she was planning to be a doctor. When she completed training and showed him her diploma, he cried. Eventually her dad came to grips with her choice of a career and was proud. He had every right to be proud. He raised a special daughter.

Another Hurt (Loneliness)

The graveside service was in honor of a 64-year-old man. He had one brother and two sons. The brother and one son came. Attendance was very small – less than 20, including some grandchildren, relatives and friends. The only emotion was from the brother. There are countless instances similar to this where families have become alienated.

One service produced no attendees at all. This individual was committed to his final resting place by four people: the funeral direction, two grave diggers and the minister. At least the cemetery workers showed respect by removing their hats as they stood by the grave before completing their job. I made a point to thank them.

Another service was for a young man in his 30's. The dad and his wife (not the mother of his children) were telling me about their family. It was a decent size crowd. The dad pointed to his daughter who was visiting with others. He said that today was the first time she had spoken to him in sixteen years. This family was facing a painful situation already. Now they were going forward with the absence of one of them. With the silence broken, it yielded opportunity for a few remarks in the eulogy regarding the value of family

It takes effort for families to gain strength from one another in the midst of grief. This is not a time to be alone. The family structure has been interrupted and being alone will rarely the result in family unity. Living in this world produces challenges and it is comforting to know we are never alone. Jesus continually stands "at the door and knocks" (Revelation 3:20). We can place our hearts in God's hand and provide and receive comfort from the heavenly Father.

Loss of a Child
When death takes a child, it creates a special kind of pain for the parent, regardless of the child's (or parent's) age. My brother's life ended on his forty second birthday. Our parents were here to deal with it. At the visitation, I saw my dad cry for the first time. He was 65.

A service was conducted for a man in his 40's. The family had faced the passing of the father two years before and the memory still was fresh. The mother's heart clearly was filled with grief.

I turned into the cemetery when I saw sister's car. She keeps the flowers fresh on the grave of her husband. It has been many years, but the void still is there. The remains of his parents are next to their youngest son. He was the last child to go away during their lifetimes. They spent their final years without their children. It must have taken a special effort on their part. Attempts at encouraging words would seem to come up short.

Loneliness, disappointment and separation are part of this broken world. It is tempting to question our own effectiveness to comfort. If we reach out to the hurting and see little (if any) response to our efforts, what have we done wrong? There is no way to fail in this if we do it with the same comfort we have received from God" (2 Corinthians 1:4). He is the master comforter and we can be effective when we place our hearts in His hand.

Can we see ourselves in the words of R.W. Long in his book *Push the Rock*? "For most of my life I have felt like I'm spiritually deficient when it comes to understanding whatever it is that God wants me to do. I often think of myself as a spiritual Forrest Gump. As a Christian, I envy those who say that God speaks clearly to them. On many occasions, I have wished God would send an e-mail, or a Face book message, or a Tweet, or text message, or even a telegram telling me what it is I am to do. Whatever it is, I'll do it because it is my earnest desire."

In Matthew 28 we find Jesus issuing the great commission to the disciples: "Then the 11 disciples went to Galilee, to the mountain where Jesus had told them to go. When they saw him, they worshipped him but some doubted." Three times, Peter (the rock) denied that he even knew Jesus. Judas betrayed Him. Jesus spent three and a half years preparing a handful of men to carry on His work when He left. Often it appeared that His efforts were producing no results at all. Neither did He escape hurt and disappointment. But Jesus looked past all of that. It's a good thing for us that He did.

Chapter 17

Where Is Dad?
"So you will walk in the way of good men and keep to the paths of the righteous." Proverbs 2:20

The question was raised at a meeting with other pastors: "What is the reaction of parents when they learn of the destructive behavior of one of their children?" One answered, "They don't care."

That is difficult to accept. Listen to a parent pour out their heart when they learn of their child acting in a destructive way. Self-blame is a temptation whether it is the result of something taught or modeled. Parents would like children to make us proud.

Prayer Requests from Young Offenders.

Regularly a chaplain shares a list of prayer requests from young men in juvenile detention. These are teenagers and younger. Spiritual issues have not dominated their thinking. Lives have been in turmoil due to dysfunctional families, inappropriate companions and other reasons that are a mystery. They now are facing the legal system, probation, perhaps extended incarceration.

The chaplain offers them the opportunity to express prayer requests and the results often are stunning:
- Pray that me and my mom's relationship falls back into place and gets stronger.
- Can you pray that I go home and become somebody in life and make people happy and change me?
- Pray that when I go to court, that whatever judge I get shows mercy and lets me go home or can you ask God to proceed in a miracle because I need to go home for my momma's health.
- Please pray for me to gain control of my anger and violence.

- Pray that I can keep from being discouraged from getting locked up again.
- Pray for my mom, who has cancer.
- Pray for my little daughter and for the family who is taking care of her.
- Pray for me to go to school when I get out of here and stay at home and not do any drugs.
- Pray for my momma's health and that when I go to court, whatever is best for me happens.
- Please pray that the judge picks a good place for me to go.

Many dads have checked out of the lives of these juveniles. This is a crucial age when they are looking for guidance and many dads are absent. The boys suffer for lack of direction and it is in rare instances that mom can do it alone.

One police call took a good part of the officer's shift. A 14-year-old girl walked out of the house and mother could not find her. The girl was a special needs child with a history of depression. Mom was raising three children alone and interaction with the siblings was impressive. They retrieved her chair to use outdoors and a jacket to keep her warm. This was a fatherless home.

Isn't this interesting? "Fathers, do not aggravate your children or they will become discouraged" (Colossians 2:21) (NIV). "Fathers do not provoke your children to anger by the way you treat them. Rather bring them up with the discipline and instruction that comes from the Lord." (Ephesians 6:4) (NLT). Notice how both passages stress the function of fathers.

A large number of police calls involving misbehavior of a child involve a fatherless home. When we arrive, often the question is asked, "Is dad around?" Many of these never would occur if there were a father in the home (not a stepfather, grandfather, uncle, or boyfriend). No one can truly replace a father in the life of a child he took part in bringing into the world.

Family courts are full of child support cases. The father shared in the child being here but many are seldom willing to pay child support – even court ordered child support. Ask any dad who has remained in their home with the mother of the child and built a strong relationship. They will acknowledge paying more child support than the father who was sanctioned by the court to do so. Also, they earned the right to be part of the child's upbringing. No dad does it perfectly. Being there and loving their mother counts for a lot.

On one police call, the youngest son was unruly and physical with some members of the family. The young man had violated his most recent probation and continually misbehaved. Yet his father continued to drain the family finances to rescue him. The older sister made the 911 call when her brother strangled her. She was asked "where is dad?" "He is in the house and won't come out." "What will dad do now that your brother has violated his most recent probation?" She replied, "He can't do anything. He's used all of his money." Trying to speak with the father was hopeless. He was totally deflated.

How Far can we take a Child?

Two brothers (8 and 6) became abusive with their mother when she kept their cell phones as discipline. The mother was asked the usual question about the presence of their dad. Those sent to that call know the answer to that question before it is asked. It has been asked to mothers, both single and married. Dad has become occupied with other matters and the mom is left alone with the kids.

At the dinner, we sat next to the juvenile judge who was the featured speaker for the evening. I leaned over and asked the judge "Can you pinpoint the main cause for lack of direction of our young people today?" The honorable judge didn't even pause to think about the answer: "The lack of a father figure in the home." That is motivation to ask the question so often when mom places a call for help with her misbehaving child. God has my heart in His hand when we enter one of these homes. I grew up in a home that was largely fatherless and can testify to the emptiness.

Balanced home life

A home is incomplete with one parent missing. Also it will be dysfunctional if the mother permits abuse from the man in the house. Children witness this and draw conclusions as to their role in relationships.

Studies by the National Center for Fathering have produced startling information regarding the absence of a father.

Children who are raised in a home with an involved father are:
- 39% more likely to earn mostly A's in school
- 45% less likely to repeat a grade
- 60% less likely to be suspended/expelled from school
- Two times more likely to attend college and find stable employment
- 75% less likely to have a teen birth
- 80% less likely to spend time in jail

In his book, "The Good Dad," Jim Daly cited United States Census figures showing 15 million kids live apart from their biological fathers. This represents one out of every three American children.

He adds that the stats are no better for girls. "They, too, struggle as kids and into childhood. Moreover, females raised without fathers are four times more likely to engage in sexual intercourse at an early age and more than twice as likely to get pregnant early." These figures are documented in their report "Fathering in America" May 2009.

The following was related by a responsible father: "It's my ex-wife's birthday today, so I got up early and brought flowers, cards and a gift over for the kids to give her and helped them make her breakfast. I'm raising two little men. The example I set for how I treat their mom is going to shape how they see and treat women and affect their perception of relationships."

Proverbs 23 is full of wisdom on behalf of parents and offspring: Verse 24 says "The father of a righteous child has great joy; a man who fathers a wise son rejoices in him. May your father and mother rejoice; may she who gave you birth be joyful." There is a vivid memory of the time I sat too long in a left turn lane after the light had changed. The man in the pickup made significant use of his horn, then drove beside me and presented me with a vulgar hand signal. His son (the passenger) looked at me through the closed window and stuck out his tongue. A mistake was made. Not the first time. It was troubling to see a young boy learn such a negative response from the man who is most important in his life.

Organizations have sprung up that provide direct contact between older men and young boys. These efforts decrease the school drop-out numbers. In addition, there are an impressive number of these boys who grow up with dreams that take them to college to achieve degrees. These boys come from fatherless homes. It is an effective effort to deal with an issue that arises from living in a broken world. Bless these adults for refusing to allow Satan to have the victory. They have placed their hearts in the hand of God.

There is the organization already mentioned that involved teaching a class of fathers delinquent in child support. After the 10-week class, it is amazing at the effect this time had in connecting those dads with their children, even though the relationship between the parents had deteriorated. This demonstrates that there is a way when the adults make a conscious effort on behalf of the children.

Parental Expectations

A counseling course divided students into triads. This was a group of three students dealing with real situations. One person would bring a struggle to class, and the other two would listen and try to help the troubled person come to grips with a solution. There were two male students and a female who was married to a medical student. One day, the lady came to class totally wiped out emotionally. Her husband's best friend (also a medical student) had taken his own life.

The lady was prompted to talk and tell what she knew. This young man had significant pressure from his father to become a doctor. It was obvious to him that his heart was not leading him in that direction. He was studying medicine to gratify his father's wishes and dreaded telling his dad of the true direction of his heart. He chose a devastating way out and our classmate's husband was suffering – not to mention the young man's family.

An interview with Duke Ellington posed the question about the difficulties he faced in his early years such like most musicians. The Duke said, "I didn't have any." "You didn't starve or suffer?" the interviewer asked. Mr. Ellington responded, "No, I started out doing what I most liked to do, working with music. I had faith in myself and it was easy. When I was a little boy, I was loved so much I don't think my feet hit the ground until I was seven years old."

He was a gifted pianist and composer and packed music halls wherever he played. Accounts of his life tell how young he was when he began excelling in music. An article related a conversation (told by the man himself) between the maestro and his father. They were discussing the work of Mozart. The conversation drifted to the fact that Mozart composed a symphony at the age of 8. Dad asked his child "where is YOUR symphony"? We have discussed instances of an absent or uninvolved father. There is another extreme. Paul wrote it two ways: "Fathers, do not provoke your children to anger" (Ephesians 6:4) and "Fathers, do not provoke your children so they will not become discouraged" (Colossians 3:21).

Imagine being the son/daughter of the Pharisee who came to the temple and prayed next to the Publican. He envisioned himself better than the man next to him. It is unreasonable to expect our children to be what WE want them to be. That is more pressure than the child can bear. Proverbs 22:6 addresses our responsibility to train up a child according to their "natural bent. That takes insight as a parent. When they make decisions that are destructive it can bring us to our knees.

There are far too many children that are products of dysfunctional homes. Some find direction and support in others willing to provide a good example. Thank God for good role models. "And you yourself must be an example to them by doing good works of every kind. Let everything you do reflect the integrity and seriousness of your teaching" (Titus 2:7) (NLT).

Father Figures Are Within Reach

My final year in the military was spent questioning the value of faith in God. A call was made to Yokohama. It was an effort to speak with the chaplain. A return to the states and civilian life was close and confusion was dominating this young man. A visit was needed with a spiritual leader and there was a willingness to make the trip to him. He asked if we could talk over the phone. That didn't seem sufficient.

When home was reached, mother's minister was sought. In the visit, he responded with his total attention. He led prayer for guidance and direction and arranged several meetings with a wise elder. The interest, attention and example of these men still remain a defining experience in the life of a person who dispelled doubts the hard way.

Here is a summary of lessons learned:
1. It is appropriate for a man to have a strong faith in God and confidence in His presence;
2. It is appropriate for a man to listen to the heart of another person;
3. It is appropriate for a man to possess and project a gentle spirit.

Upon discharge from the military, another gentleman took me to a local golf course and taught me how to swing a club. It was encouraging when the minister extended an invitation to play every Monday. Often the choir director joined in. Dad took me to a few car races and air shows. Not one word about God or becoming a responsible man.

Dad's youngest son was a bit of a disappointment when he decided to enter the ministry. Dad resented church. As a child, he had a bad experience in parochial school. Mother dealt with his anger each Sunday when she headed for church with her young children. One Sunday, the man was so angry he grabbed the left front fender of the 1946 Pontiac and completely ripped it off. This was a horrible vision for the young children in the car. The trip to church was made anyway – with the car missing a fender.

There are fathers in honorable professions whose children make the same choices for themselves. Humility would be appropriate as well as thanksgiving. Walking in the steps of Jesus is a significant challenge. There are no perfect children. Neither are there perfect parents. We run this race together.

It was her first Father's Day without him. She walked by and the urge to speak was strong. Her dad had been a friend longer than she had been in this world. She was assured that the family was being remembered. The exact words escape, but it was something like this: "We dads want you to miss us being here. But it is most important to us that we set a good example for you. ." That wasn't learned ONLY from a book. It came from living, being a dad and knowing what a child misses when dad is not around. Also, it came from growing up around good men and women who reached out to someone who needed guidance (Proverbs 2:20)

It has been said that a person cannot give to another what he does not have himself. Examine the history of a delinquent dad and what led to his delinquency might be evident. It would be a bonus to see gentleness, goodness and leadership modeled by the right person. But Proverbs 2:20 offers assurance that it is fine to receive these qualities from someone who is respected and has placed their heart in the hand of God. Thank God for them.

Chapter 18

Explaining the Unexplainable

"Don't be afraid. Just stand still and watch the Lord rescue you today.... The Lord himself will fight for you."
– Exodus 14:13, 14 (NLT)

Life consists of many unexplained experiences. Some of them describe deliverance and rescue. Please forgive me for relating a few.

Not much is recalled about that night, sometime in 1960. Neither my friend nor I went many places alone. We joined the Navy together. Following basic training and a two week leave we were assigned to an aircraft carrier in Long Beach, California. We did most everything together – but not this time, and I don't recall why.

I left the ship and took a taxi to a club in Los Angeles where great music was played. I was under age so alcohol was not the driving force. A conversation was initiated with a civilian guest at the same club. We both liked the music and talked about a long list of subjects.

At the end of the evening my new acquaintance offered me a ride back to the ship. It was late and I was careful not to violate curfew. As we walked around to the back of the building (supposedly to his car), I was surprised when he began hitting me in the head with his fists, knocking me to the ground. We were alone and I pretended to be unconscious. It is unknown what kind of damage he could do beyond what already had been done. He began looking for anything valuable I might be carrying. My wallet was concealed but he took my watch-a high school graduation gift from mother.

My assailant gave up and walked away, leaving a young sailor saying on the ground-injured. Other people passing by was a sign that it might be safe to leave. A cab was called and the night was over.

That has been the only instance of physical violence and has not been a good memory for me. Years have left questions regarding how often this person initiated this kind of behavior. Was this the beginning (or continuation) of a life of crime for him. He was in his twenties. Parents of this individual come to mind as well. Were they aware of his choices? Was he a product of a dysfunctional home? Did he learn this behavior from companions? My hope is that he found a better and more responsible way to live. The apostle Paul did.

It occurred to me that I survived an experience many have not. It is a horrible memory and this is the only account given since it occurred. There is no "delete" button to remove this from my life story. There is no evidence that God turns his back on some people and rescues others. Elijah searched for God in a whirlwind but found Him in a whisper. Jacob found Him in his dreams. Moses found Him in a burning bush. The writer of Hebrews encourages us to "Not neglect to show hospitality to strangers, for by so doing some people have shown hospitality to angels without knowing it" (Hebrews 13:2). God has a way of bringing good from bad.

Stranger in L.A

The military transport plane had been disembarked in northern California. A train trip to the L.A area near the bus station was next on the way to the home of friends in an outlying city. It was the middle of the night and there was confusion by being in a strange new location. The heavy suitcase added to the challenge. The Navy uniform was evidence of a traveler. About a block from the destination total exhaustion forced the suitcase to rest on the sidewalk. A sizable gentleman walked up behind and said "Let me help." He picked up the suitcase, carried it across the busy street and sat it down near the entrance to the bus station. He left before he could be thanked. How he appeared when he did still is a mystery. So are the timely appearances of helpers throughout scripture.

It Happened in Paris
Brenda and I had spent a few days in London on a company trip. One of her life dreams was to visit Switzerland. A friend had been to Zermatt many times and formed a relationship with the family who owned a small hotel in Zermatt. We made arrangements to go there from London carrying far too much luggage. The flight took us from Heathrow to De Galle Airport in Paris. This was before cell phones and internet and phone rooms were available at airports. We headed straight for it. Already gone a week we missed our children. After the call and tears we dragged our luggage to the subway entry across the street. We knew where we were going but had no idea how to get there. Walking down the long subway ramp a nice gentleman (not even a Frenchman) stopped and offered help. After we reviewed our itinerary with him he pointed us toward the correct subway with clear directions. Our helper reached into his pocket and took out more than enough French currency to pay our fare. This amazing dream was made even more amazing by the unidentified helper whose kindness was unexpected.

Who Handed Me That Money?
With encouragement from a supporting church in Tennessee and a group of new Christians in Wisconsin, we made a move to serve this new church there. With no working funds and no personal assets, it was a significant mystery how our family would find housing or contribute to this infant church.

Staying with one family after another didn't provide much stability. Once we stayed with a lady who was caring for an elderly relative. Feeling in the way would be an understatement. Totally dependent on other people, I took a guilt trip and chastised myself. Perhaps this was related to 1 Timothy 5:8: "Anyone who does not provide for their relatives, and especially for their own household, has denied the faith and is worse than an unbeliever." It was obvious whose job it was to care for my family and the quality of that care was questionable.

Chances of finding a house to buy seemed slim. No financial resources existed. The church had a reception for the family from Texas. At this event a church member walked up to me, introduced himself and placed a significant amount of cash into my hand. It was in September, so perhaps a tax deduction was being sought – He was a CPA. He explained that the money was to assist in securing a home for this family. This good man placed no conditions on the use of the money and he made it clear that it was NOT a loan.

An Offer Accepted
Driving in the area where we would be working, an older home (built in 1890) appeared with a "for sale" sign in front. Someone was in the yard. Stopping revealed it was the owner – not the real estate agent. As we talked, I asked him the price. He gave me a much lower amount that was being asked and agreed to take it. The next day a call was received from an angry real estate agent. The owner insisted on going forward with his agreement.

Reduced Rent?
We made the transition from ministry to business. Having lived in a home owned by the church, moving would involve finding a house on our own. Insurance sales had been a part time effort and seemed to be working but there was no history of success to offer a landlord.

In the search for a place to live a house was located in the same area. The owner listened to our dilemma then made an astounding offer. He arranged a significant reduction on the rent for six months. This was another mystery but additional evidence that God cares for us (1 Peter 5:7).

Rescue in Venice

We were on a Mediterranean cruise with a group from church. This was a dream since age 17. After checking into our hotel in Venice, Italy we left to fulfill one of our dreams - a Venetian gondola ride. We booked it ahead but had a terrible time locating the place to catch the gondola. Locals were very unhelpful- possibly due to the language barrier.

After creating that memory, we attempted to find our way back to the train station that would take us to our hotel. We boarded a water bus that took us the opposite direction. Finally heading the correct way, we questioned which stop to disembark. Again—very little help.

A gentleman with his family overheard our desperation and came to our rescue. He took pity on the couple from Texas and said "just stay with us. We are going to the same place." Trusting (as well as desperate), it was late in Venice, and the body clocks were on Texas time. We left the water bus with this family and followed them to the ticket kiosk at the train station. He purchased tickets for his family of five and two more for the couple he just met. Two families navigated back to the hotel and crashed from exhaustion.

Not only were we all staying at the same hotel, we all were going on the same cruise. We exchanged contact information and this man has been thanked for his kindness many times.

Where is Mr. Horton?

Brenda and I were asked by the mother of one of our grandsons if we would take him into our home. Providing for him had become a challenge for her. We insisted on securing court documents in order to provide all of his needs – from education to health care. Soon we sought medical assistance from the state and it was granted. We received and submitted required documentation. Response was slow and we continually were told that the papers did not arrive or were incomplete.

We called and asked if we could hand deliver them and were given an address. The address given was not even close to the correct destination. Another call yielded additional incorrect directions. Still another call reached a gentleman who identified himself as Mr. Horton. Explaining our unfortunate situation frustrated him. He recited the correct address and said he would be waiting in front of the building when we arrive. He smelled of cigarette smoke as we followed him up to his desk. A commitment was made to relieve the confusion by transferring the case to his charge. He did that and everything ran smoothly.

When it was time to renew we needed an answer to a question. Mr. Horton's extension was called. A female caseworker answered and explained that there was no Mr. Horton in the office. The grandson turned 19 and coverage terminated.

Continual prayer was offered that we might have a more active role in the life of this grandson. God brought that about. There were heartaches and challenges along the way but God has been faithful to open doors that would not have been open otherwise. We are never in need of evidence that He cares for us (1 Peter 5:7).

Grace We Don't Deserve

Psalms 107 is another narrative of the history of God's people told centuries after it happened. It is an account that the Israelites have heard all their lives. The writer concludes "…those who are wise will take all this to heart; they will see in our history the faithful love of the Lord."(verse 43) It is obvious that God never provided protection, security and guidance because His people were obedient and deserving. They rebelled many times and Moses stepped in to defend them. God was fully capable of wiping out the entire nation and starting over. We don't deserve it either.

Think back on your life. How many near misses can you recall? How many unexplained victories? God can rescue a prostitute and place her into the family tree of Jesus. He can cause a young boy to defeat an enemy giant with a sling and one stone. He can open the doors of a prison so His servants can carry on His work. He can bring about reconciliation between two brothers who had every reason to be alienated for life. He can turn His face away from His only son as He hung on the cross for the sins of unworthy humans. There is significant value in remembering.

During these challenges we received comfort from God through others that we want to return and are willing to place our hearts into God's hand.

Chapter 19

Priorities learned from Pain

"One of the men lying there had been sick for thirty-eight years. When Jesus saw him and knew he had been ill for a long time, he asked him, 'would you like to get well?'" (John 5:5) (NLT).

When we face sickness or injury, wellness is our goal. Is that correct?

If we recover what will we do with the days we are given? How will our time be used? Will we take our place on the couch in front of the television? Will we search for opportunities to renew our hobbies, addictions, find new ones or travel the world? Is that all there is to a healthy and fulfilling life?

Frequent news from the inner circle reports news of declining health or the passing of a classmate. Good health is a blessing and periodic exams bring comfort. But the results of an EKG led to the following words from the primary care physician: "This is not good." The test revealed a trial fibrillation. Blood thinners were ordered. The hospital was next (outpatient) with two procedures. Improvement resulted, but blood thinners are daily routine.

A CT scan to evaluate a hernia revealed much more. A total of six defects were revealed, ranging from cysts on the liver, to an enlarged spleen. Is it the beginning of the end?

It seems we are eventually confronted with our mortality. Earth is not a permanent residence for any of us. "Our citizenship is in heaven" Philippians 3:20. This has produced a great deal of introspection of how time is spent. A graveside service was conducted for a dear 84-year-old lady. She had not achieved greatness by the world's standards. She never went to college. It was an inspiring day to listen to her six children share heartwarming memories of mom sewing their clothes and making clothes for their dolls. Her husband had been married to her for 63 years and still was deeply in love with her.

Receiving More than We Ask

An account of God's generosity is found in the account of Solomon becoming King. He received an offer from God Himself. In a dream God said, "What do you want? Ask, and I will give it to you!" (1 Kings 3:5). Knowing he was assuming the role of king his response to God was "give me an understanding heart that I can govern your people well and know the difference between right and wrong" (verse 9). God promised to give Solomon what he requested. He also vowed "I will also give you what you did not ask for—riches and fame! No other king in all the world will be compared to you for the rest of your life" (verse 13). Solomon was given far more by God than he requested or expected.

This 92-year-old gentleman was happy to receive a wife 63 years ago. It was clear to him that he received much more than expected. He went on and on about the virtues of this woman that were not obvious to him when they married. The children related much more. How many of us have experienced God's generosity in similar ways? In the beginning there is not even a glimpse of what will be experienced over the next several years.

Another account of the will to live is found in the life of King Hezekiah (2 Kings 20). Hezekiah became deathly ill and the prophet Isaiah was sent to him with a message: "This is what the Lord says: Set your affairs in order for you are going to die. You will not recover from this illness."

"When Hezekiah heard this, he turned his face to the wall and prayed to the Lord, 'remember, O Lord, how I have always been faithful to you and have served you single-mindedly, always doing what pleases you.' Then he broke down and wept bitterly. However, before Isaiah had left the middle courtyard this message came to him from the lord: "Go back to Hezekiah, the leader of my people. Tell him 'this is what the Lord, the God of your ancestor David, says: I have heard your prayer and seen your tears.

I will heal you and three days from now, you will get out of bed and go to the Temple of the Lord. I will add fifteen years to your life and I will rescue you from the king of Assyria. I will defend this city for my own honor and for the sake of my servant David.'"

First, dying at this time was not in Hezekiah's plan. He had plans. Second, God can take what appears to be a terminal situation and turn it around. Third, God just may have His own agenda in granting these additional years and Hezekiah fit into His plan. We never can underestimate God.

God's plan or ours?
There is much about life that gives us a false sense of control. When we flip a light switch we expect the room to light up. Turn the ignition key and we expect the car to start. We expect hot water to come from the faucet when we turn the left handle. What if it doesn't? There are power failures, car batteries die and water heaters fail. The failure of any of these is an inconvenience and reminds us of how little control we have of our lives. None of these are terminal. But they certainly put us out of our comfort zone for a while.

That is the effect of sickness. It has a way of changing our plans. In most cases, we will respond to a change in our physical condition by seeking treatment. We educate ourselves on symptoms of various conditions and seek medical attention at their onset. Dealing with any serious illness tends to instill fear in us and those close to us.

In the book "How to Live 365 Days a Year" (2002) by Dr. John Schneider, he reported that over 60% of those who see a doctor are there for a real illness – however it is a reaction to emotional stress. He referred to this as EII (Emotionally Induced Illness). His discovery was intriguing, as well as his courage to discuss it.

The scriptures declare "A happy heart makes the face cheerful" (Proverbs 15:13) (NIV). If this is true, then the converse must be true as well. This issue was being discussed in a church bible class in which one of the students was a medical doctor. The doctor was quizzed about agreement with Schneider's conclusion. The answer was an emphatic "yes."

There is little question that the spirit of a person's response to emotional stress affects physical health. A counselor confirmed that symptoms are real. A chiropractor once suggested that the most common issue he treats is pain between the shoulder blades in the center of the back. This is a real symptom and often referred to as a "target organ."

God's plan for our life challenges is no mystery. A.W. Tozer wrote in "Paths To Power," 31,32): "The fallow field is smug, contented, protected from the shock of the plow and the agitation of the harrow…But it is paying a terrible price for its tranquility: Never does it see the miracle of growth; never does it feel the motions of mounting life nor see the wonders of bursting seed nor the beauty of ripening grain. Fruit it can never know because it is afraid of the plow and the harrow." The psalmist wrote, "It is good for me to be afflicted, that I might learn your statutes." (Psalm 118:71). The writer of Hebrews (5:8,9) said of Jesus "Although He was a son, he learned obedience through what he suffered." God's agenda for our lives is likely different from our own.

Do We Really Want To Get Well?

Why would Jesus ask such a question? The man had been incapacitated for much of his life. He had come to a place that was believed healing could occur, yet it had not happened for him. Do you get the urge to look at Jesus, frown and wonder why he would ask a question like that? Who wants to be sick and stay that way?

The lack of the best health has advantages. Brenda has undergone knew surgeries. Each time the doctor asked if we would like a temporary handicap placard. There is a small fee but it certainly was a benefit. Confession time: It was nice to park close to the entrance of a store. It took knee surgery to earn that privilege.

One police officer is sensitive to the unauthorized use of those placards. He goes through parking lots to check their validity. If it has expired, he intercepts the driver when they return to the vehicle, confiscates the placard and issues a citation. His explanation is that there is a victim to this offence and that is the person who really needs the parking space.

There is a harsher opinion. Suppose a person is overweight because of neglect or poor choices. One officer said harshly that these should be required to park the farthest distance from the front, leaving the closer spaces for those who truly are disabled. On a trip to a store with a family member there were no carts available. The clerk noticed a gentleman who was by the register when she asked him if he still needed the cart. He stepped off and said "no, I was just tired."

Attention is given to a sick person until wellness is declared. Madeleine L'Engle wrote, "One cannot be humble and aware of oneself at the same time." "A man's pride will bring him low, but a humble spirit will obtain honor."(Proverbs 22:4). We can make good use of our time of wellness and God will be honored when we place our heart in His hand.

Examining Priorities

Prior to obtaining his PhD Jess Lair owned an advertising agency. He admitted he worked too much and allowed his ego to get confused with his possessions and life style. A heart attack at a young age produced an examination of priorities. He went back to college, earned a doctorate in psychology, moved to Montana to teach in the university and wrote a few books. This resulted in time to focus on his family and provide stability for them that had been lacking. He did not spend time regretting the past. Instead, he focused on how he could best use the present time to make a difference.

That's a real hero. Most of us have made mistakes we regret, can learn from them and redirect our lives. Dwelling on them could cause us to grieve ourselves out of existence. A good man once said "it is partially because of the mistakes I have made that I can relate to others who have are discouraged or distraught." That is wisdom and that is a heart in the hand of God.

Jess Lair was clear when he said 'I NEED MY MISTAKES.' James discussed the subject of wisdom (James 1:5ff). Proverbs 2 gives a long list of assets derived from wisdom and wisdom often is learned from our mistakes. It would be a shortcut and bonus to sit at the feet of someone and learn from their mistakes. But most often we do not allow ourselves that convenience. That brings us back to the question: "if we are sick and seeking healing, what will we do with the time we are given, if recovery is granted?" Will we return to our previous life, neglecting the same things (or people) as before, stroking our ego in the same ways? What would be the purpose of the reprieve from sickness? Hezekiah was told he would be given fifteen more years. He might have had in mind how he would spend this reprieve, but God had an assignment for him. It is appropriate to listen, with our heart, to the prompting of the heavenly Father. He knew us before the universe was formed (Romans 8:29), knows us better than we know ourselves and is our best resource for how to spend the time we are granted.

Chapter 20

What is a Christian?

"God saved you by his grace when you believed. And you can't take credit for this, it is a gift from God. Salvation is not a reward for the good things we have done, so none of us can boast about it."
– Ephesians 2:8 (NLT)

Jess Lair had a point. When someone asked if he was a Christian, he would reply, "I'm working on it." It was Luke who wrote, "When you have done everything you were told to-do, you should say, we are unworthy servants; we have only done our duty. (Luke 17:10).

A good daughter gave account of her dad's life after he passed. "He lived his faith." That is a fine tribute from the daughter of a dad who lived 88 years. Matthew 15:8, Isaiah 29:13 (NLT) contain strong words: These people "honor me with their lips, but their hearts are far from me. James 1:26 (NLT): "If you claim to be religious but don't control your tongue, you are fooling yourself, and your religion is worthless." Titus 1:16 (NIV): "by their actions, they deny Him!!" Scripture is full of these descriptions. Who do you know who "lived their faith?"

Randy Harris, in his book *Soul Work,* wrote "What lies behind everything I've said, is the fundamental conviction that being a follower of Jesus Christ has very little to do with going to church and a great deal to do with the transformation of our lives. And unless we start living qualitatively different lives in the world, the message that we speak has no credibility."

It is not uncommon for a person to write their own obituary. For those who do there is a personal choice of life interests to list. There is nothing wrong with golfing, hunting, fishing, traveling, sports or being a fan of a particular sports team. Those are temporal and short lived. Even those dedicated to those interests exhibit deeper traits that require the heart and those are the things that leave a legacy.

It is interesting to note what certain persons have chosen to have engraved on their head stones. James Dobson told of his mother's humor. Once she suggested the phrase "I told you I was sick" be engraved on hers. Mel Blanc (the voice of Bugs Bunny) had these words engraved on his headstone: "That's all, folks." How about Frank Sinatra: "The best is yet to come." Or Merv Griffin: "I will NOT be back after this message." Humor can serve up to the end.

"He stretched others." How about that for a headstone? Most of us have been influenced by others with large hearts. Reaching out to us certainly earned them no financial reward or name recognition. Usually there is no intentional plan to take us under their wing. We were not a project to them. It is moving to observe godly character in another person and desire that for ourselves. Jesus is not here visibly but scripture encourages us to embody the attitude of Jesus.

In 2 Corinthians chapter 5 Paul discusses matters that have been a mystery to mankind for centuries. Where do we go when we leave this life? What will we look like when we get there? Will we have a body? Will we know one another? The list goes on. In verse 6 he states "so we are always confident, even though we know that as long as we live in these bodies we are not at home with the Lord-for we live by believing and not by seeing."

As long as we are here, we are working on our responsibilities as a Christian. How about you? It's worth the effort. It can be done during a golf game, hunting, and fishing (etc., etc.,etc. Surely a deeper meaning can be located within these activities. The promises are appealing and the message of salvation can be shared in whatever activity we are in.

Faith of Abraham, Noah, et. Al.

The world we live in is not compatible with the concept of going forward with no direction or assurance. We like to know where we are headed before we strike out. There are certain sales professions that work with projections of results based on activity. . It was Steven Covey who wrote *Seven Habits of Highly Effective People.* It became an essential manual for anyone who wanted success from their efforts –from commission sales to churches. One directive for any person or organization is to create *a* "Purpose Statement." Churches and businesses adopted this practice and it became a direction declaration. This, in no way, removes God from the equation. We know His will and the result He desires. We don't always have the direction for the vision we pursue but He does.

Hebrews is a book of encouragement, especially chapter 11. A study of the first verse gives special insight. "Faith is the confidence that what we hope for and assurance about what we do not see," (NIV) For years, the original word translated "assurance" was found only in this verse with no other presence in biblical or secular literature. In an archeology dig, a skeleton was discovered, along with a briefcase that contained legal documents. . The skeleton turned out to be that of an attorney. He was representing a client when Rome was confiscating real estate from citizens who could not document ownership. One document in the brief case was a title deed supporting ownership of his client. This discovery gave new understanding to the passage. Faith is the proof of ownership of the promises of God by His obedient followers. There is no wavering, no doubt that these are ours.

In this chapter, Abraham is depicted as one who received a charge from God to go to a land he was going to inherit. God gave no travel map, directions or daily schedule. But, according to verse 8 Abraham "… went without knowing where he was going". And even when he reached the land God promised him, he lived there by faith-for he was like a foreigner, living in tents" (verse 9). Abraham had periods of doubt, and we can identify with those. After all, how many men are promised to become a father at age 100? We are just as susceptible of falling short as Abraham. Most of us have encountered some amazing Christians along our journey. But none of them would be bold enough to declare that their faith has been without struggle.

Risk is present. A faithful Christian couple had two children. Their world was upended when one of them died at a young age. Sometime later, their other child lost his life in an accident. There was another incident that was devastating. It involved a young child. Each parent understood the other had retrieved the child from the family vehicle on a hot summer day. Actually, neither had done so. When he was discovered first responders were unable to revive him. The officer speaking to the media stated "this is not something that will happen to the majority of us, but it happens enough around us to call attention to the situations we need to be aware of with our own children." This world produces challenges to the faith of God's people.

We can question the goodness of God or take accountability ourselves. It was "….by faith that Noah built a large boat to save his family from the flood: (Hebrews 11:7). He warned the world but only had influence over his family. Faith stories from individuals are stunning and intriguing. It is an inspiration to meet those who are willing to share. They have a way of enriching our walk with God. They have begun with the end in mind and trusted God for direction. That is the heart that God asks us to place in His hand.

Keep Walking

Gideon had issues walking by faith. God called Gideon a mighty warrior and was called to deliver Israel from the hands of the Midianites. The only assurance Gideon was given was that God would be with him. Gideon still needed more assurance. Twice, Gideon placed his fleece before God for a sign that he could count on God's presence. Gideon sought assurance by his own standards. Beginning with thirty-two thousand men, God reduced that number to 300. Gideon was victorious and there was no question that victory came with the help of God. It was unorthodox. The army approached the Midianites with torches in one hand and trumpets in the other. For special effects, they smashed clay jars. This confused the Midianites and they turned on each other. God also brought down the walls of Jericho in an unorthodox manner. His people marched around the city seven times. After this, they shouted and blew trumpets. What kind of military strategy is that?

Can we identify with Gideon? How many times have we wanted to solicit the fleece and receive assurance that our faith was pushing us in the right direction? Then we are taken back to Abraham who was directed to go to an unfamiliar place. He hoped against hope, becoming a father at age 100, and the head of a nation that established the bloodline for the birth of Jesus Christ, God's ultimate promise to the world. Abraham truly walked by faith and left us a supreme example.

It takes strong faith to strike out in a direction with no assurance. But God's presence is amazing. The details were seldom known or how they would be manifested. Throughout eternity, Jesus knew that His sacrifice would be significant but the human part of Him dreaded it. He prayed "If you are willing, take this cup of suffering away from me. Yet I want your will to be done, not mine" (Luke 22:42) (NIV). It never hurts to ask.

Gideon was slow to trust- but he achieved victory in a completely unorthodox manner and with fewer resources than he thought were needed. God made up the difference. Gideon went on to govern God's people and was better qualified for that position because of his faith.

Examine the struggles of God's faithful servants throughout history. Job suffered tremendously. Joseph struggled for over 20 years. Some struggled far less than anticipated – sometimes far more. But in each account, we see God given credit for victory and they were better at the end. We can begin with the end in mind then trust God to provide the details to get us there. It's always better when God is there.

Chapter 21

The Story of Our Lives
"Does a young woman forget her jewelry, a bride her wedding ornaments? Yet my people have forgotten me days without number." - Jeremiah 2:32 (NIV)

A bride retains memory of her wedding garments her entire life. A 22-year old searched for the perfect wedding gown, and then came across the gown worn by her grandmother when she married her high school sweetheart in 1962. After some restoration and repair, the bride surprised her grandmother by walking into the rehearsal dinner in that special dress. It was emotional for both of them. The memories were more precious because this grandmother had become a widow not long before.

It is intriguing how our past affects us. There are good and bad memories that follow us through life. They impact how we think and handle situations as adults. There are horrible memories as a young person waking up in a home with no heat, electricity or water. It was more hurtful knowing mother and sister would be without these conveniences – especially on a day with freezing temperatures outside. Dad failed to pay the utility bills. He had his own agenda and it did not include being with his family or providing for them. The paycheck of a 13-year-old provided some relief when a part time job was found. Years of marriage produced a family that never once was deprived of utilities in the home. Past experience shaped the future.

A friend attended a seminar conducted by a psychologist. At one point, attendees were asked for a show of hands if they had been touched inappropriately as a child by an adult. It was estimated that over 80% of the hands went up. That kind of child abuse is not new, it just went unreported and not discussed. But is can shape trust in others. It is possible to build a life in which this story can be rewritten. There are many of us, like Jacob after wrestling with the angel, who are walking with a limp.

The account of Joseph in Egypt has some merit in the life of someone attempting to rewrite their story. Joseph was number 2 in that country (only below Pharaoh) arriving at that position after over 20 years of suffering. He was in charge of distribution of the considerable food resources during a famine that affected his family back home. They came to Egypt and were sent to Joseph. Not knowing who he was, Joseph was cautious before revealing his identity to them. He was the youngest and treated horribly by his brothers. He was bold to assure them "you meant it for evil, but God meant it for good." Joseph understood that God was forgiving and he wanted to experience healing in his family.

Comfort resulted when these brothers joined together in releasing the past. It assures that it can be done. We seek forgiveness for hurtful things done and set out on a new path. We depend on God's spirit for strength and His grace in the midst of our imperfections. Christ paid the price for our shortcomings and we have every right to rejoice in His forgiveness and place our heart in His hand.

Releasing the Past
Some things are precious and worth holding on to. Isn't it inspiring to listen to an elderly person detail something that happened on their youngest child's first day of school? What makes it amazing is the difficulty they have in recalling something that happened yesterday.

Israel continued to complain to Moses. It didn't take them long (even fresh from victory) to bring up the past and their vision of the past was not good. These were not very forward-looking people. They complained to Moses, "Why have you brought us out of Egypt to die in the wilderness? There is no bread! There is no water! And we detest this miserable food" (Numbers 21:5) (NIV). A life of slavery was better?

There is no benefit in glorifying the past. It was Paul Harvey who declared "Tomorrow is my favorite day."

Tomorrow is my favorite day,
I would not look the other way.
As time goes forward in my mind,
I do not crave a gaze behind.
My greatest hour is yet to be,
Marking time ahead of me.
Calling me to travel on,
And set my compass toward the sun.
There's nothing in the past for me,
But that which served to set me free.
To walk the upward pilgrim way,
Longing for the better day.
The past I'd rather leave behind,
The present challenge who can find?
Tomorrow is my favorite day,
I would not look the other way.

Peter conveyed hope when he wrote: "So be truly glad. There is wonderful joy ahead" (1 Peter 1:6) (NLT).

Chapter 22

Distraction of Vanity

"Don't think you are better than you really are. Be honest in your evaluation of yourselves, measuring yourselves by the faith God has given us." -Romans 12:3 (NLT)

Greek literature is an intriguing study. From Dante's inferno to Achilles' heel, world culture bears the influence of the days when writers created stories and characters that have left a lasting influence. One was Narcissus. He was extremely handsome and was captured by his good looks when he saw his reflection in the water. He became enthralled and stared at the image until he died. Narcissistic personality disorder is a real issue. It is a mental condition in which people have an inflated sense of their own importance and value. It can lead to troubled relationships.

The comic strip Peanuts has been around a long time. An article once revealed that Snoopy has assumed over a hundred identities – from the world-famous surgeon, hockey coach, advice columnist, novel writer (who never seems to get past the opening remarks), a bald eagle, the Statue of Liberty, skating pro, WWI flying ace to Joe Cool. There always seems to be a character he would rather be than himself. In the above passage, Paul directs us to measure ourselves "by the faith God has given us." That standard is sufficient.

For most of us humility and self-acceptance comes and goes. A car salesman explained his method of convincing a potential buyer. They would come to him with their heart set on a specific car. The salesman would take them for a test drive. His normal route was the business district of the city, which contained several high-rise buildings covered with glass. As they passed those gleaming buildings, he would capture the attention of the prospective buyer and point to his reflection in the glass and comment, "Look over there at how cool you look driving this car." That alone closed most sales.

Paul cautioned that vanity is not the measure of our lives. It is interesting how our culture has equated our value with certain items. From clothes to automobiles to homes to places of travel, marketers have proved that vanity sells. Families overload themselves with debt to impart an image seeking to gain acceptance or appear to rise above the status quo.

It is estimated that less than 30% of all off-road trucks are driven off-road. Why do we spend so much of our time posing, rather than projecting the image of who God created us to be?

A fairly new word in the English language is the word "selfie." Young people take selfies with the duck face and two fingers in the "victory" position next to pursed lips. We can take selfies repeatedly until we are satisfied that the image is worthy of being posted on social media.

Have you noticed walls at the gym are covered in mirrors especially in the weight lifting area? It is amusing to see someone watching themselves as they lift. What is the correct name for a mirror used by someone to apply makeup? Vanity?

An interesting call to police was placed by an observer across from a small gathering. The caller had captured a phone recording of a male strangling a female a few feet from the crowd. Officers detained them both, handcuffed the male and placed him in the car. The female was asked to sit on the curb. I asked permission to speak with her. She was the girlfriend and had just informed him she was carrying his child. That angered him – so much that he had his hands around her neck. "How long have you two been together?" She replied, "Two years." "Has he behaved this way before?" She said, "I've never seen this side of him." There was a temptation to say many things but the temptation was suppressed. Either there was a good job of posing or she ignored the danger signals. Perhaps both.

Posing becomes a distraction that can rob us of a spiritual focus. Paul wrote "Don't copy the behavior and customs of this world, but let God transform you into a new person by changing the way you think. Then you will learn to know God's will for you, which is good and pleasing and perfect" (Romans 12:2)(NLT). He goes on to say "Do not think of yourself more highly than you ought, but rather think of yourself with sober judgment."(Verse 3).

It's such a distraction to spend time being fake, looking for the world's approval. God created us each unique. Giving attention to that image will bring Him glory and peace to our hearts. Can we concentrate on that together, touch lives in a special way and leave this world better off than we found it?

Posing
John Eldredge calls it posing. Our great granddaughter once was in our kitchen being held by her dad. She was fussy but I wanted a photo anyway. When the camera was pointed at her, she launched into a big smile. That did not represent her attitude at the moment, but it was a photo worth keeping.

Photos from the past depicted family members with serious faces. That doesn't happen much anymore. We want to look our best so a smile comes before the snap.

Maybe appearances are why we reply "fine" when someone asks how we are. We want to appear to others that we everything in our lives are going well. Jeremiah cried out to God. "I am ridiculed all day long; everyone mocks me" (Jeremiah 20:7). We want to avoid being mocked and appear in control and be seen as we want to be seen-not as we really are.

A study was done long ago of the most psychologically well-adjusted people in the world. It was reported that symphony orchestra conductors topped the list. Can you imagine waiving your arms toward those surrounding you and having them respond to your direction? Having everything go my way certainly has not brought out the best in people. Struggling against challenges and enduring hardship has.

It took Joseph 22 years to prepare for the outcome that God had in mind. He ended up as Number Two in Egypt (under Pharaoh), but most of those years were spent with his life on the line. How can we expect anything more?

Jesus warned about projecting a false image. In Matthew 6:2, He says, "So when you give to the needy, do not announce it with trumpets, as the hypocrites do in the synagogues, and on the streets, to be honored by others." He condemned false displays of righteousness when He said "Everything they do is done for people to see. They make phylacteries wide and the tassels on their garments long" (Matthew 23:5) (NIV).

Why are we not content with who we are? "Whoever wants to be my disciple must deny themselves and take up their cross daily and follow me" (Luke 9:23). There is nothing wrong with "who we are." There is danger in attempting to be someone we are not. Look closely at the lives of those who are most often imitated or copied. Are their lives truly better than ours? Do we know their entire story?

The false image and the real person always are at odds. More effort is required to project a perceived image than to develop what God placed in us to begin with. John warns "Dear children, keep away from anything that might take God's place in your hearts" (1 John 5:21).

Look at a group photo that includes you. It is not uncommon for our eyes to go directly to the spot where we are standing. When we are asked regarding the welfare of our children, do we present them as a disappointment?

As a funeral service is prepared, the closest family member usually is contacted. With the help of other family members, they produce a list of traits that celebrate the uniqueness of that person and how they stood out to them. I always wonder how often these family members communicated those qualities and values to that loved one while they were around to hear it?

When we draw our last breath, our glory will not be based on how well we have copied the life and achievements of someone else. God created each of us with a gift and instructs us to "use them well to serve one another" (1 Peter 4:10)(NLT). No one else can be us. He can do amazing things with our hearts if we let Him.

Chapter 23

Learning the Hard Way

"Jesus told him, 'Stand up, pick up your mat and walk.' Instantly the man was healed! He rolled up his sleeping mat and began walking!" – John 5:8, 9 (NLT)

It's the way most of us learn -including me. I entered college looking for my questions to be answered. A wise professor responded to a question for a direct answer by looking directly at the inquiring student and saying "We are not here to give you answers. Our job is to teach you where to go and search for the answers." The silence in the classroom was overwhelming.

I never took a class from the dean over the graduate school, but we became good friends and preached for neighboring churches. On a visit to his office one day, I asked him for a quick answer to the meaning of a passage. Rather than giving an answer, he replied, "That's a good question. I'd like you to write a research paper on that subject and tell me what you learn." That was not the response sought from the dean, but it was a good one and opened a door for a life of learning. Not long after that, he was approached with another question. Often, we are slow to learn.

It was an undergraduate biblical professor who thrived on brief, to-the-point research work. He assigned a research paper once a week with instructions to limit the paper to three typewritten pages-not two and a half or three and a fourth, but exactly three. It became a lesson in extreme discipline to say what needs to be said and not waste words.

The following quote is attributed to Michael Jordan: "I've missed more than 9,000 shots in my career. I've lost almost 300 games. 26 times I've been trusted to take the game-winning shot and missed. I've failed over and over and over again in my life. And that is why I succeed."

The most valuable lessons of life come the hard way. Paul thought so, "I have learned the secret of being content in any and every situation, whether well fed or hungry, whether living in plenty or in want." Philippians 4:12 (NIV) Paul had learned a great deal and it came to him the hard way. Paul's next statement is captivating: "I can do all this through him who gives me strength" Philippians 4:13). How did he receive the strength: Through divine revelation? Heavens no! Standing over the spot in Rome designated as this apostle's final resting place, the silence is stunning and this man's history shouts. That is why Brenda and I agreed to name our only son after him. The apostle Paul learned a great deal by experiencing hardship. So do we.

Weeping with Those Who Weep

As a minister working with the police, a lot of time is spent in the passenger seat of a police car. More than once I have heard a question from the left seat: "Where is the fairness in life?" The answer goes something like this: "I don't know. It certainly has eluded me." When we are overwhelmed, Job stands out as a hero. Proverbs 2:20 declares "...walk in the steps of good men." Job is a worthy mentor. We cannot go wrong responding to hardship with him as our example.

Confession time. I often wonder how effective I am at reaching out to someone who is hurting. That issue came when the officer and I went to the county hospital to guard a female who was around 50, although her lifestyle made her appear much older. She was there because she had plans to jump off a building and end her life. In between nurse visits, the officer encouraged me to talk with her.

"My name is Tom. I am a minister and here with this officer- what is your name?" No response. Her arm band had her name and date of birth. Direct eye contact was made as she lay secured to the gurney by a single handcuff.

"Jill (not her real name), I see your name is Princess Jill. You are more important than we expected. My boss sent me with a message for you." Her eyes locked with mine. "My boss is God. You are extremely valuable to Him and that is why you have been given the title 'princess.' My boss loves you. You are His daughter and he is sad when you think about hurting yourself." She needed medical attention and was taken to another part of the hospital. That is when we walked away and God was asked to take over.

At such a time the most effective comfort for us is a word from God. The officer recognized my dilemma and walked out with me with his hand on my shoulder. It was clear that Jill did not need advice on how to get through it all- especially if the person giving the advice has not experienced anything similar. She needed to know that she was valuable and her life mattered. I never have located the words to do that. All I can do is place my heart in the hand of God and trust He will provide words that are appropriate.

In New Testament times, often mourning was done in an organized way. Part of the process was to hire professional mourners. These people could express grief over the death of another person without even knowing who they were. Although it added to the atmosphere of grief, it was difficult to imagine it was very effective. Those who help the most always are those who knew the deceased personally and could give accounts of memories.

We look for the right words to reach out to those who are hurting. Often silence is the best choice. Janey was a wife and mother. Her husband and two children were hospitalized at the same time-her husband with a life-threatening heart condition. She didn't need an attempt by anyone to make a sympathetic phone call but was not certain what she needed from anyone else. It is a point of limbo.

Value of Time

Jim Croce was 29 when his music took off. *Bad, Bad Leroy Brown* was elevating his success and sending him on a demanding concert schedule. He was missing his wife. His hit song *Time in a*

Bottle had become a great sing along piece that carried a significant message.

Jim Croce died in a tragic plane crash in Louisiana at the age of 30 leaving behind a wife and son.

I write this in the aftermath of the passing of my friend Kenny and now my older sister. I was asked to deliver the eulogy for both. Time was our ally for many years. It served its purpose and it now is time find a way to move on. All that is left are memories and how the influence of those relationships had a part in shaping me.

When Solomon became king, God offered to grant him any request. Solomon simply asked for wisdom and knowledge to serve effectively. God gave Solomon much more. All I expected from Kenny was friendship and a big sister in Betty. I received much more. Similar to David and Jonathan (1 Samuel 18:1), Kenny and I became one in spirit. I have loved him as myself and that was returned. When he told me he would not be receiving any additional treatment for his cancer, I apologized to him for spending all those years without discussing spiritual matters. That changed and we both spoke the words "I love you" many times and shared confidence in God's forgiveness. We anticipate the continuation of this friendship in a new place where brokenness will not distract.

Two officers and I arrived on scene. A young boy turned his car at a busy intersection and struck an adult on a bicycle. He stopped and we were right behind him and there before an emergency call could be made. The bike rider needed no medical attention. Even with a superior officer, blame could not be placed. A conversation was initiated with the boy and his mother. Both were distraught. It was a good time to assure him that the officers were commending him for stopping to check on the bike rider. No one could be cited for negligence. Mom and I agreed that her son would remember this experience for a long time. It would help shape his future as a driver and as a person. As we were leaving, the boy reached out to shake my hand and his mom thanked me for "the kind words."

They were not mine. That was a good memory for the officers and me.

The intention was to speak something comforting at a stressful time. Much more came from this experience than anticipated. That is how life has played out with the God of Abraham, Isaac, Jacob and Tom.

Chapter 24

I Don't Have Time for This

"... there is a time and a way for everything, even when a person is in trouble" -Ecclesiastes 8:6 (NLT)

He is one of the godliest men you ever would meet. He is generous, loving, and merciful and comes from a godly family. He can be trusted to do what he says. At breakfast, we opened our hearts about the heaviest burdens we are carrying. There is no safer place to talk about these things. Thank God for a trusted brother.

He shared his diagnosis. His doctors had a plan but it will seriously interrupt his own plans. Not long ago he dedicated his life to full-time ministry. This will change things. He didn't hold back when he said "I don't have time for this." That was an appropriate response – and honest.

Challenges never come at a convenient time. A published police memorial was a moving tribute. An officer lost his life at the hands of a person full of hate. This left the officer's children without a father. When he left that morning, he made it a point to kiss his children and tell them he loved them. Families of police officers are aware of the dangers they face each day. Nevertheless, they live with the assumption that Daddy will be coming home at the end of his day. It is a shock of unimaginable proportions to receive word that he won't be coming home. These children will go through school, graduate, begin a family and have children who only will hear stories of their grandfather.

It is a tragedy that this father was taken from his children. He WAS involved with their lives. But God will compensate for that vacancy. There are "good men" (Proverbs 2:20) who are willing to fill the void. No one can fully replace the father God gave us. But there are generous hearts that are willing to take on an additional assignment. Peter referred to Mark as "my son" (1 Peter 5:13). Paul called Timothy his son (1 Timothy 1:2), and Titus (Titus 1:4) and Onesimus (Philemon 1:10). "The Lord blessed Job's latter days more than his first" (Job 42:12). The loss of a father need not have the final say.

A friend told of his dad leaving for the military at the beginning of the Korean conflict. His dad never returned. Both he and his brother grew up without a dad and both thrived in the medical field. The absence of a father did not stop their lives. Another friend tells of his dad passing in his thirties and my friend was preschool age. He has spent years working with boys who are missing a father and are in trouble with the law because of their behavior.

My dad lived to be 76 but essentially, I grew up without him. He was gone a lot. But when he was home, he was not attentive to his children. The excessive use of alcohol led us to prefer his absence. We were growing up and didn't have time for this. He left for good when his children were very young. Home life was hard but peaceful.

A sad obituary was published: " Albert passed away on ……..., which was 29 years longer than expected and much longer than he deserved…..He leaves behind two relieved children….along with six grandchildren and countless other victims including an ex-wife…At a young age, Leslie quickly became a model example of bad parenting…and complete commitment to drinking, drugs, womanizing and being generally offensive… Albert's hobbies included being abusive to his family, expediting trips to heaven for the beloved family pets and fishing Albert's life served no other obvious purpose. He did not contribute to society or serve his community and he possessed no redeeming qualities, besides quick-witted sarcasm which was amusing during his sober days… With Albert's passing, he will be missed only for what he never did; being a loving husband, father and good friend…No services will be held, there will be no prayers for eternal peace and no apologies to the family he tortured…Albert's passing proves that evil does in fact die and hopefully marks a time of healing and safety for all."

Imagine the effort it took for Albert to be that bad. It was Mark Antony who said of Julius Caesar at his death: "The evil that man does lives after him; the good is oft interred in his bones." Pain and heartache indeed live on in the lives of victims. Albert (like all of us) was given an entire lifetime to make choices that left a positive legacy.

Another family published their mother's obituary: "In ---- she became pregnant by her husband's brother. She abandoned her children…who were then raised by her parents…She passed away on ---- and will now face judgment. She will not be missed by her children, who understand this world is a better place without her."

In 2 Chronicles 20,21 we meet Jehoram. He became king. He was "32 years old when he became king and reigned in Jerusalem eight years. No one was sorry when he died."(2 Chronicles 21:20) (NLT). None of us want that as an epitaph. We can be better stewards of our time.

The Baggage we carry

Reports continue that the divorce rate both inside and outside of church is a consistent 50%. Police officers have told of a training class in police academy in which their spouses are involved. During this class, they are warned that many would be affected by the stress of the job and in danger of their marriage ending within five years. Some have said they went home with their spouses and committed to beat the odds. Reports show the presence of a traumatic experience increases the divorce rate to 80%. Included is the disability of a spouse, death of a child or an indiscretion on the part of one of the spouses.

A police officer friend was 50 when he married. I joked, "Maybe it would be best to wait until fifty to marry in order to dispose of baggage." He smiled and said, "Because we waited, we brought a lot of baggage with us."

Couples grow in their relationships with time. Gary Chapman refers to the first two years of marriage as "the tingles." The tingles are replaced by deeper things that have the ability to sustain the relationship. That is the purpose for the vows in the beginning. Our vulnerability never escapes God. Validation from the heavenly father comes from humility; "Humble yourselves before the Lord and He will lift you up" (1 Peter 5:6, James 4:10).

Brenda and I often visited my sister in the rehab facility. It is inspiring when her roommate's husband came to dinner with his wife who is a dementia patient. He pushed her to the dining room in a wheel chair, cut her food and fed her one bite at a time. It is likely that if the situation were reversed, the wife would be just as attentive. It is an inspiration to watch that kind of response to a commitment made years ago – long after the "tingles" have vanished. It is a clear example of someone who has placed their heart in God's hand. .

It Keeps Coming

We were asked to pray for a young person with a special need. A rare disease resulted in the amputation of both legs below the knees. A subsequent request was to pray for an additional surgical procedure that would remove both arms. The request was that the amputation be below the elbows. It worked. The prayers continue, only now the request is that God will reveal himself in this experience and His glory will have an everlasting effect on the family. Those not affected are free to go about our daily routine and shudder whenever the thought crosses our mind. Certainly, it is an opportunity to consider Romans 8:28, "We know that all things work together for them that know the Lord".

Let's not stop there. Verse 29 tells us "For God knew his people in advance and he chose them to become like his Son, so that his Son would be the firstborn (supreme) among many brothers and sisters." We need look no further for the desired outcome of any suffering experience. There is no evidence that God "zaps" us with hardship. He knows our world will produce these events. His promises take us through them with the goal of being more like his Son. Being lord of my own life won't work- never has-never will. Jesus is the only one worthy of that honor and being like Him is the Father's ultimate goal for us.

Matters such as these receive no press. Yet the media becomes obsessed with the misbehavior of a celebrity. A child can be taken from this world prematurely and God is chastised.

Often it's best to keep issues close to home. It is frightening to think what social media might do with instances of "off the charts" suffering. Those who strike out at God's goodness appear to be confident in their conclusions. It doesn't change things. It makes more sense to reconcile the presence of a loving God in the face of suffering. No human has demonstrated confidence in their own ability to navigate life alone at the helm.

While Brenda was confined to the cancer floor, I made my daily visits to the coffee shop across the street in the children's hospital. That trip cannot be made without being surrounded by parents and their children who were there for treatment of diseases that were interfering with their lives. Parents were unable to work, often traveling from their home in another town. Often the children react violently to treatments. We cannot escape the presence of suffering. It is all around. When we accept the existence of God our faith is stretched on a daily basis. But with God, there is hope.

David related the value of suffering: "My suffering was good for me, for it taught me to pay attention to your decrees" (Psalms 119:71). The writer of Hebrews wrote that Jesus "learned obedience by what He suffered? (Hebrews 5:8). He gave His perspective of these experiences: "...this will be your opportunity to tell rulers and other unbelievers about me." (Matthew 10:16-18).

We are not immune to persecution for following Jesus (2 Timothy 3:12). Neither are we protected from the things that characterize the world in which we live. Sickness and death are all around. Innocent people suffer. Our bodies are not made to last forever and they usually develop issues far sooner than desired. A pastor who studied Human anatomy and Physiology related touring a Dissection Laboratory at a medical college. Upon entering, a sign captured his attention: "THE SPIRIT OF LEVITY IS NOT PERMITTED IN THIS ROOM! AS YOU ARE, THESE ONCE WERE, AND AS THESE ARE YOU SOON WILL BE!" A stunning source of inspiration is to be exposed to someone who finds joy in the midst of pain.

No credit could be found for this statement: "...there are horrors no human heart is equipped to bear." It is comforting to know that we are not expected to bear them alone. "Give all your worries and cares to God, for he cares about you" (1 Peter 5:7).

Chapter 25

Peacemakers

"Blessed are the peacemakers…" Matthew 5:9 (NIV)

It is beyond the average thinker how police officers spend their work week doing what the job requires. There are occasions when an officer will locate a missing person, help someone to a safe place after an accident or give a lost and distraught person a ride home. They have been known to change a tire on someone's car in the cold. It is moving when an officer attempts to pay for his meal and the cashier informs him someone paid it for him. I insist on paying for dinner when I am with them but often there is resistance. But I am good at persistence.

A tragic experience can linger in my mind for weeks while they seem to run together in the mind of a police officer and that experience has left the officer's memory. They are focused on the task at hand and able to make the transition from one call to the next without much thought. Individuals who do this work have a divine gift.

Much of what is witnessed during a shift of responding to calls is someone taking something that is not theirs, causing harm to another person or damage to property that is not theirs. Often these are actions that cannot be reversed. Damage endures for a long time. Proverbs 22:3 (NLT) declares "A prudent person foresees danger and takes precautions. The simpleton goes blindly on and suffers the consequences."

Behavioral Consequences

During a shift we were riding through apartment complexes looking for an individual the officer had dealt with previously. He brought up the suspect's photo on the computer screen in the car and explained that this man had knocked out all of his girlfriend's teeth and she was hospitalized. "And she still is his girlfriend?" I questioned. I grew up around domestic violence and determined not to copy that behavior. I married a girl who was the only girl in a family of six kids. She can handle herself. Honestly, I never had the courage to give it a go.

The officer had detained a male who had assaulted his pregnant girlfriend. She was packing her things and leaving. We commended her for having the courage to take a stand against abuse. The male was sitting in the back seat of the police car and the officer was talking with him through the window through steel bars. He is a dedicated husband and father and was having a hard time talking with the offender. Standing a few feet away, he motioned for me to come to the window. He wanted me to talk with the subject, first explaining that I had been married longer than he had been alive and never assaulted my wife. I began questioning him and his motives pointing out that the unborn child's mother honored him by carrying his baby and staying with him to share parenting duties. Now it may be over for the three of them. He began to cry and see his behavior as permanent damage.

An officer's training only subsidizes his heart in the work he/she does. A local hospital kept a list of ministers to call when needed. The regular chaplain was receiving cancer treatment. It was an honor to be on call to intervene at crucial times. Once, a call came asking for help in a situation no one likes. A young man was driving on a trip with his mother. He had been sleeping in the back seat as his mom drove. She became very tired, woke him, and asked him to drive. A few minutes after they returned to the road, he fell asleep, the car wrecked, and his mother did not survive. The highway patrolman who worked the accident gave a briefing prior to entering the ER where the young man was being treated. We stood beside this young man as he lay on the hospital bed. The patrolman did a masterful job explaining the outcome to the driver. More education was dispensed that day than could ever be in a formal way. That is part of the job description of these peacemakers in uniform. It is clear why scripture refers to them as "children of God."(Matthew 5:9).

An Officer's Perspective

A very fine officer raised a familiar objection during a shift. It is a familiar issue. "I don't claim to be religious, and there are some issues that make no sense to me. I look at all of those who are suffering (including children) and it is puzzling. I have a friend who has been fighting cancer and it appears she is losing. We deal with a lot of head–on car crashes that are alcohol related and in most of those (if there is a fatality) the intoxicated driver is the one who survives.

It was obvious where he was going because most of us have had the same kind of thoughts. I completed his thought: "If there is a God who created the universe and he loves us and has the power to prevent this kind of evil, why doesn't he?"

"Exactly."

I explained that I returned from the military with severe doubts about the existence of God. After undergraduate work, the opportunity arose to study Christian Apologetics at the graduate level. I needed to make sense of all the hurt and pain in a world created by a God who has the power to stop it. It seems more reasonable this way: *Let the bad things happen to evil people and leave good people alone.* That makes more sense. Looking directly at him with a conclusion deep from a heart that understands where the officer was struggling, I said. "My answer is I DON'T KNOW." For someone who spends his work days around people who choose evil, their struggle with this issue makes sense. Most of us have faced the same question. Daily they encounter others who choose behaviors that hurt themselves and others – hurt that cannot be reversed. The perpetrator must live with that decision for the remainder of life.

There are officers who see God's way as the only reasonable choice. Some have shared painful experiences that were survived by faith in God. One officer voices a prayer for blessing before his car leaves the sector. There are those who pray with victims in distress. God oversees this work.

Peacemaking comes in all Forms
Incarcerated juveniles are invited to submit new prayer requests to the chaplain, who shares them with supporters:
- I hope and pray that my mama become un-incarcerated and can get me back home.
- Pray that my uncle gets out of prison and that I can go home before Thanksgiving.
- Pray that I can go home with my family to help my mom to take stress off of her.
- Pray that my granny gets better, and for God to watch over my family. And be with me and my brother on our court dates.
- Pray that I will not get a determinate sentence to JJD, (Juvenile Justice Detention). Also bless my family and the ones I dislike.
- Pray for me to go home and for my sister to get out and never come back.
- Pray for my family, my case, and for a second chance.
- I pray that I can be in my son's life and be a better man in life.

The only way the past will serve these young offenders, is to bring about a better future. It is expected that they will walk into their future with a limp. But Jesus paid a high price to offer us a better future. There is no question that Jacob (Israel) made good use of his life despite his limp (Genesis 32:31).

The officer related what was going on. He had a man handcuffed in the back seat of his car. Jeff had harmed himself several times leaving injuries on his head, face and arm. He blamed himself for several things that had gone wrong in his life. Before backing away from the open door, the officer told Jeff "there is not anything that can't be forgiven." Jeff needed to hear that.

Leaving the door open and no place to sit, I took a knee.

"Jeff, I'm a minister and work with these officers. My boss has sent me to you with a message. Do you know who my boss is?" A finger rises from cuffed hands and points upward. "You are right, Jeff .. My boss sent me to tell you how valuable you are. You are far more valuable than you think and every time you hurt yourself he hurts too."

Jeff had made some statements to the officers indicating he had a spiritual perspective. Taking a chance, we discussed Satan's work and how he was the real enemy, not Jeff. We prayed right there as Jeff squeezed my hand with both of his. We commanded Satan to leave Jeff alone in the name of Jesus Christ. Heaven will reveal the outcome of this encounter but God certainly found an assignment that night for a willing heart.

A girl in her middle teens reported an assault on the school bus. When we arrived, another officer and two ambulance attendants were in the living room. Mom was weak from chemotherapy and the daughter was demanding to be taken for medical attention, even after the EMT (upon careful examination) assured her that her nose was not broken. A trip to the hospital would place mother at risk since she was weak and would be around other sick people. The girl could not go without her mother and the EMT informed her that her condition did not justify a ride to the hospital in the ambulance. The young girl was wearing an ankle monitor having been on probation since the age of twelve. The ambulance attendants told her that they were receiving other calls and needed to go. It is amazing how some mothers are mistreated by their own children, Mom being a cancer patient changes nothing.

Upon leaving the scene, the mother was backing out the family car to honor her daughter's demand.. Rebellious teenager wins again. Families (as well as communities) are left with scars.

In an obituary a brilliant man's family related his own admission regarding his addiction. It was the outcome of a life less than what he had imagined. By his own admission, he allowed his light to go out by failing to live the life of which he was most capable.

What are we expecting from life anyway? Comparing our lives to others usually will leave us feeling deficient. We don't know the whole story of anyone else. It is shocking news when a young celebrity (or relative of a celebrity) takes their own life. They live in the limelight and the demands become overwhelming. Let's start with Psalms 23:1 and make the Lord our Shepherd. From there it is promised that we will lack nothing.

On a call with an officer, we entered an apartment. What we encountered would break the heart of any parent. Father and son were sitting on the couch. The son was deceased. I followed the father out the door, pleading to God for words of comfort. My heart was touched when it became evident that my son was near the same age as this father's son. God had my heart but my effort felt limited, since the words did not come from an emotional level that matched that of the grieving father. It rarely does.

Words of comfort are not learned from books or college classes. The Crisis Intervention classes provide limited skills needed to comfort a person who is in the first moments of a crisis. Severe crisis (often without warning) are part of living in a broken world and it won't stop until our lives do. Knowing that does not reduce the hurt. Officers continually issue the reminder that the best education comes from being out there when the need arises. The 8 eight-year-old boy in the back seat is being cared for by first responders. He just made another effort to end his life. The frantic mom was in the driver's seat. She rolls down her window and we pray. She is commended for the behavior of the other two boys in the car. She is a good mom and needed to hear that.

We only can bridge the gap between the hurting person and the only one who has the ability to bring comfort. Life has no "search" mechanism that yields instant answers. Neither is there a "delete" button that will erase mistakes, or their consequences. God is the master teacher. He walks through the fire with us when we ask and often when we don't ask.

We live in a broken world and are subject to hurt. But as long as grace and forgiveness abound, we can endure. Satan will have success for a time, but we know the final outcome: "Every knee will bow before me; every tongue will acknowledge God" Romans 14:11 (NIV) Philippians 2:10,11.

Chapter 26

Where Do We Go From Here?

"We must quickly carry out the tasks assigned us by the one who sent us. The night is coming, and then no one can work." John 9:4 (NLT)

1 Kings 19 is an intriguing account. Elijah was chosen to deal with King Ahab and his wicked wife Jezebel. But Elijah was a bit of a whiner. Why would anyone with an assignment directly from God complain? Ahab was a wicked king with a wicked wife. That is quite a combination for a position of leadership, isn't it? Just read the account in 1 Kings 21 of Ahab taking the vineyard of a good man, Nabal, just because he wanted to. It's enough to make your blood boil.

Nothing Elijah told Ahab was received with favor. Ahab and Jezebel couldn't wait to get their hands on this man of God and silence him forever. Everywhere Elijah turned, he was met with resistance and God found him sulking. Ahab and Jezebel had threatened his life, "Elijah was afraid and ran for his life. When he came to Beersheba in Judah, he left his servant there while he himself went a day's journey into the wilderness. He came to a broom bush, sat down under it and prayed that he might die. 'I have had enough Lord" he said. 'Take my life. I am no better than my ancestors.'" Even after three powerful demonstrations of God's presence, Elijah whined, "I have been very zealous for the Lord God Almighty. The Israelites have rejected your covenant, torn down your altars and put your prophets to death with the sword. I am the only one left and now they are trying to kill me too.'" (Verses 10-14).

The story ends in victory, God won and Elijah made history. You would think that if God were going to send Elijah on such a mission, He would "Make straight paths for him" like He did for John the Baptizer whose job was to prepare for the coming of the Messiah (Isaiah 40:3; Mark 1:3). But even with the "straight paths," John was put in prison for his efforts and eventually beheaded. How fair is that? There is no promise in all of scripture that guarantees smooth sailing for those carrying out God's mission. There is a promise we can count on: "Everyone who wants to live a godly life in Christ Jesus will suffer persecution. But evil people and imposters will flourish." (2 Timothy 3:12,13).

Life Perspective

Aristotle is given credit for teaching Alexander the Great. History bears witness to Alexander's accomplishments. At the age of 25, he had conquered much of the known world. Now he found himself on his deathbed at 33.

Summoning his generals, he made three requests:
1. The best doctors should carry his coffin.
2. The wealth he had accumulated should be scattered along the procession to the cemetery.
3. His hands should be left loose, hanging outside the coffin for all to see.

One general had the courage to request an explanation. Alexander explained:
1. I want the best doctors to carry my coffin to demonstrate that, in the face of death, even the best doctors in the world have no power to heal.
2. I want the road to be covered with my treasure so that everyone sees that material wealth acquired on earth, stays on earth.
3. I want my hands to swing in the wind so that people understand that we come to this world empty-handed and we leave this world empty-handed after the most precious treasure of all is exhausted, and that is TIME.

Are Our Days Numbered?

Scripture addresses the subject of time. Psalm 90:12 (NIV): "Teach us to number our days that we may get a heart of wisdom." James 4:14 (NIV): "What is your life?... you are a mist that appears for a little time and then vanishes." John 9:4 (NLT): "We must quickly carry out the tasks assigned us by the one who sent us. The night is coming when no one can work.

John Lennon is given credit for the quote: "Time you enjoy wasting is not wasted time." Maybe it's just me. I've always felt a strong stewardship of time. Fishing, golf, television, and table games are relationship activities. You won't find me installing Christmas lights in the front lawn because I enjoy doing it. Brenda has a beautiful Christmas spirit and she likes it. Isn't it more blessed to give than to receive? Am I not to "consider others as better than myself?"(Philippians 2:3). It is truly rewarding to receive Father's Day and birthday cards from children and grandchildren with memories of time we spent together. What we did stands out in their history. It is motivation to step forward and create more.

In Mitch Albom's book "The Timekeeper," we read, "Try to imagine a life without timekeeping. You probably can't. You know the month, the year, the day of the week. There is a clock on your wall or the dashboard of your car. You have a schedule, a calendar, and a time for dinner or a movie. Yet all around you, timekeeping is ignored. Birds are not late. A dog does not check his watch. Deer do not fret over passing birthdays. Man alone measures time. Man alone chimes the hour. And, because of this, man alone suffers a paralyzing fear that no other creature endures. A fear of time running out."

My friend was right. Our hearts are drawn to something (or someone) that is lost or didn't turn out as we envisioned and diverts our attention from others who depend on us. It is devastating to pour our hearts into the life of a child or grandchild only to watch them make a life decision that results in irreversible consequences. Nearby there are other precious lives and time is on our side – at least for a while. An adult choice is needed. Mitch Albom is right.

"We yearn for what we have lost. But sometimes we forget what we have."

It was Barbara Bush who said, "At the end of your life, you will never regret not having passed one more test, not winning one more verdict, or not closing one more deal. You will regret time not spent with a husband, a friend, a child, or a parent."

Message of the Firehouse

Pain will remain. The things that bring pain are not going away as long as there is time. But God has made plans for us to survive and thrive and get to the other side of our pain and maintain our value to others.

At the age of 18 I arrived at the Naval Air Station in Atsugi, Japan, where I would spend two years. The leadership was big on fire prevention since aircraft were in constant motion. Passing by a miniature fire station on a pole captured my attention. A sign on front contained these words: "Open this door and see the number one fire prevention tool known to man." I could not resist. There was a mirror placed in the back of the firehouse, I was looking at myself, and the message was clear. Owning up to responsibility for behavior has been a constant in my life. There has been no one else to blame for mistakes or bad choices. How could anyone argue with the message of the firehouse? "The person who sins is the one who will die." (Ezekiel 18:20). Thank God for grace.

Most of us have made choices that brought pain to ourselves as well as others. Harry Truman sent a clear message with the sign on his desk said, "The Buck Stops Here." It is common to listen to an offender in the back seat as he is being transported to jail – blaming someone else for what he/she did to get arrested. A juvenile's prayer request asks "Please pray for me to go home because it's not my fault I'm in here." A treasured gift is forgiveness, but it is like removing a nail from a post. The nail can be removed, but the hole remains. We can choose our behavior but not the consequences –and often they are lasting. The only place to turn is Christ, but we must take the first step.

It bears repeating: Pain won't go away in this life. It is a challenge to join with David and say, "It was good for me to be afflicted so that I might learn your decrees" (Psalm 119:71) (NIV). It also is a challenge to follow the directive from James: "Consider it pure joy, my brothers and sisters, whenever you face trials of many kinds because you know that the testing of your faith produces perseverance…Let perseverance finish its work so that you may be mature and complete, not lacking anything." (James 1:2) (NIV).

Aesop wrote, "Better to be wise by the misfortunes of others than by your own." Does someone we love need to accommodate us by suffering so that we can learn God's decrees and grow character? Who can argue that we come out on the other side of pain with character strength that would not come any other way?

C.S. Lewis wrote, "Hardships often prepare ordinary people for any extraordinary destiny." Those who inspire the most always have their own accounts of overcoming. Hearing them gives us a heavenly perspective. Again, Lewis wrote, "Aim at heaven and you will get earth thrown in. Aim at earth and you get neither." The apostle Paul wrote, "I consider that our present sufferings are not worth comparing with the glory that will be revealed to us." (Romans 8:18).

A famous quote by Charles Spurgeon goes: "A Bible that is falling apart usually belongs to someone who isn't."

A message on the back of a T-shirt said, "Finish empty." What a great epitaph! It was the very thing Jesus said as He addressed the Father in John 17:4 (NIV): "I have brought you glory on earth by finishing the work you gave me to do. "The means of doing so might include playing golf with a lonely person, being available to someone struggling with grief, providing financial relief to someone who really needs it, touching the life of a student who is receiving little encouragement from those he loves, or listening with our heart without offering advice or a comparable story. There is no limit of what God can accomplish if we are willing to place our hearts in His hand.

A bold commendation is given to Joshua in Joshua 11:15 (NIV): "As the Lord had commanded Moses his servant so Moses commanded Joshua, and so Joshua did. He <u>left nothing undone</u> of all that the Lord had commanded Moses." That is a stunning tribute to anyone at the end of life – he "left nothing undone."

Joe Buzzello wrote in his book "A Life In Sales," "Character is formed (and success attained) when you run the long race. Are you willing to FINISH?" That is a worthy pursuit in any endeavor – including life. Let's join with Paul who wrote with confidence: "I have fought the good fight, I have finished the race and I have remained faithful. And now the prize awaits me – the crown of righteousness, which the Lord, the righteous Judge, will give me on the day of his return." (2 Timothy 4:7,8) (NLT).

Death Changes Things

It was the second death call within a week. Coming home to find her companion unresponsive on the floor forced this person into unfamiliar territory. It's not a daily occurrence for anyone. Our lifestyle or expression of faith did not match, and that was acknowledged. Also, it was agreed that the pain of separation from someone we love was not foreign to the police officers or me.

A few days later, a funeral service was conducted for a grieving family facing a future much different than their past. Death is part of living in a world into which sin was introduced (Romans 5:12). Death was not a familiar experience for Eve. That made it easy for her to be tricked by Satan's lie when he said "You will not die" (Genesis 3:4).

Grief is difficult but has value. In John Eldredge's book *All Things New*, he writes, "The thing about grief is it opens the door to the room in your soul where all your other grief is stored – which can be a good thing if you handle it well, take the opportunity to heal the neglected grief. But still, life begins to feel like it is only and always going to be loss."

What life "feels like" and "is" are two different things. Paul wrote, "The Lord is faithful and he will strengthen and protect you from the evil one." (2 Thessalonians 3:3) (NIV). God's children believe it, continually experience it and observe it in the lives of fellow believers. This is the message to the hurting as we (together) journey onward.

Finding Strength

The Apostle Paul was on a mission and nothing stopped him. He listed for the Philippians many of the hardships he endured to accomplish his mission. Nothing mentioned was pretty, but he made the best of those challenges. He wrote from prison, "I have learned to be content whatever the circumstances." (Philippians 4:11-13).

Wouldn't it be great at the end of life to confidently say to God, "I have brought you glory on earth by finishing the work you gave me to do?" There is no greater legacy. Jesus showed us how and confirmed it to the Father. He is our model. The Message translates 1 John 3:2 this way: "All of us who look forward to his coming stay ready, with the glistening purity of Jesus' life as a model for our own."

Paul's accounts give us a perspective that will carry us through life. This won't plague us forever, "God shall wipe away all tears from their eyes; and there shall be no more death, neither shall there be any more pain; for the former things are passed away." (Revelation 21:4) (NIV).

John Eldredge wrote: "The human heart and soul are imbued with a remarkable resilience. But they are also very fragile, for we were made for the habitat of Eden and not the desolation of war in which we now live."

The Gift of Presence

In the book "It's Your Call," Gary Barkalow wrote, "God has set this whole story up, and He must and will speak personally to us regarding our part in it." (Page 170). We have a great example in Jesus who "grew in wisdom and in stature and in favor with

God and all the people." (Luke 2:52) (NLT). Those are divine standards – adequate for this world – and will work for us as well.

He was a humble family man who made a tremendous impact in the church. His occupation – garbage collector. He loved his work, co-workers, and customers. He was a man who clearly placed his heart in God's hand. Though he has been gone a long time, his family is a living testimony of the influence of his heart. Paul had an impressive resume. In 2 Corinthians 11:22,23 he outlines his qualifications: A Hebrew, an Israelite, a descendant of Abraham, and servant of Christ. But those qualifications didn't exempt him from being put in prison, being whipped "times without number" and facing death. Rather than showcase his talents, he declared, "I would rather boast about the things that show how weak I am." (Verse 30). His resume would not land him a preaching job in our day and time, but he declared that strength came from his weakness.

God wrote His story long ago and gave us vital parts. Playing our part likely will result in discomfort and struggle along the way but result in joy. Moses, Joshua, Joseph, David, John the Baptist, Jesus, Paul, and Peter followed God's purpose for their lives and it came with significant hardship along the way. But, as C.S. Lewis once said, "Getting over a painful experience is much like crossing monkey bars. You have to let go at some point in order to move forward." Forward is the direction that will take us to our part in God's story and reveal our purpose.

We conclude with a statement by John & Stacy Eldredge: "The gift of presence is a rare and beautiful gift. To come unguarded, undistracted–and be fully present, fully engaged with whoever we are with at the moment." Your heart in God's hand can build a bridge between the hurting and the God who cares.

Summary

During a routine visit to the oncologist, Brenda and I braced for the next round of treatments. Instead, he told us she could stop her chemo because there no longer were any signs of her illness. Ezra 9:8 says, "we have been given a brief moment of grace." We went to the chemo room and hugged and thanked the nurses. They surrounded Brenda for a photo with a large hand-drawn sign that said "NO MO CHEMO." Margaret Mitchell said, "Life is under no obligation to give us what we expect." Then Staci Eldredge wrote, "God drops things into our laps just at the right time."

A hero of mine is my maternal grandfather. He was orphaned at 14 with two younger sisters. He got them into an orphanage, where they grew up to earn college degrees and work for the university until retirement. He visited our home in Texas from Tennessee when I was 5 and took me to town for the day, pouring his heart out to me and making me feel important

Five months after his visit we were in Tennessee attending his funeral. Two ministers conducting the service did their best to console a grieving 6-year-old as they rotated me from one knee to that of the other. A grandmother enduring the effects of cancer was a brutal sight for a sixth-grade boy. My brain could make no sense of it, but Leonardo Da Vinci said, "Tears come from the heart, not from the brain." That makes sense. God is eternal and His impact is eternal. He is willing to partner with us – His children. Please join me in putting our hearts in His hand. God will make effective use of our effort, others will be comforted and encouraged, and He will receive the glory.

BIOGRAPHY

Tom Montgomery is a Navy veteran. He married Brenda three years after being released from active duty. That union has lasted more than 50 years. Tom received his Bachelor of Arts degree in Biblical Studies and his Master of Arts degree in Philosophy of Religion and Apologetics in preparation for the ministry. After several years in full-time ministry a sales career brought the couple to retirement. Tom is adamant that he never left the ministry but built his business with love for people rather than sales skills.

Tom and Brenda live south of Fort Worth, Texas, close to their entire family. The family includes three grown children, seven grandchildren and five great grandchildren.